D0909267

EDGARTOWN
𝕱ree 𝕻ublic 𝕷ibrary

A GREAT BOOK should leave you with many experiences, and slightly exhausted. You should live several lives while reading it.
— William Styron

Presented by

WITHDRAWN

* * * * * *

Do Not Return

58 North Water St. ⚓ P.O. Box 5429
Edgartown, Mass. 02539

Edgartown PUBLIC LIBRARY

~ *Captain's Wife* ~

TITLE

Comments

Please share your thoughts about this book with
the next borrower. Thank you!

_____

_____

_____

_____

_____

_____

_____

_____

SEAFARERS' VOICES 7

Captain's Wife

CAPTAIN'S WIFE

Narrative of a Voyage
in the Schooner *Antarctic*
1829, 1830, 1831

Abby Jane Morrell

*Edited with an introduction by
Vincent McInerney*

Seaforth
PUBLISHING

This edition copyright © A Vincent McInerney 2012

First published in Great Britain in 2012 by
Seaforth Publishing,
Pen & Sword Books Ltd,
47 Church Street,
Barnsley S70 2AS

www.seaforthpublishing.com

British Library Cataloguing in Publication Data
A catalogue record for this book
is available from the British Library
ISBN 978 1 84832 125 0

All rights reserved. No part of this publication may be reproduced
or transmitted in any form or by any means, electronic
or mechanical, including photocopying, recording,
or any information storage and retrieval system, without
prior permission in writing of both the copyright
owner and the above publisher.

The right of Vincent McInerney to be identified as the author
of this work has been asserted by him in accordance
with the Copyright, Designs and Patents Act 1988.

Typeset and designed by M.A.T.S. Leigh-on-Sea, Essex
Printed and bound in Great Britain
by CPI Group (UK) Ltd, Croydon, CR0 4YY

Contents

Contents

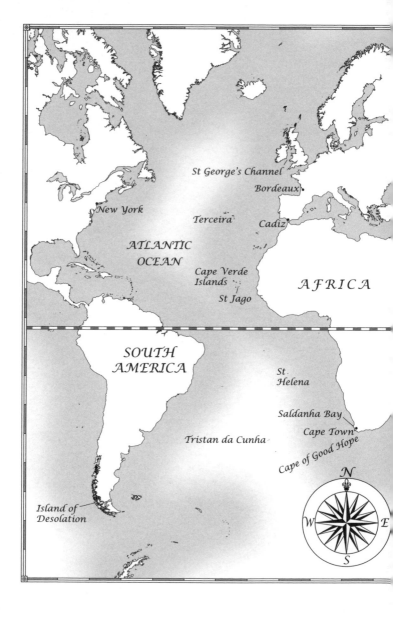

Editorial Note

THE TEXT USED for Mrs Morrell's account is that of the 1833 Harper, New York, edition. The original is said to have been ghostwritten by Samuel Knapp from a memoir prepared by Abby Morrell. This was approximately 67,000 words, reduced here to around 40,000. Losses have mainly been religious and evangelical matters of perhaps limited interest to the majority of a contemporary readership, plus some topographical and geographical material. Spelling and punctuation have been modernised.

Introduction

'I have a horror of death; the dead are soon forgotten.
But when I die they'll have to remember me.'[1]

DURING THE NINETEENTH century it became increasingly
common for merchant service masters to take their wives
to sea, particularly in the whaling industry, where
voyages of two or three years were not uncommon.
Reflecting the sailor's traditional dislike of women on
board – seen as unlucky by the superstitious and dis-
ruptive by the more rational – these ships were derisively
dubbed 'Hen Frigates'; although they have been the
fashionable subject of academic interest in recent years,
there is not much published literature by the women
themselves, and the wealth of journals are little known
and not easily accessible. Among the first, and most
accomplished, is Abby Morrell's account of a voyage
between 1829 and 1831 that took her from New England
to the South Pacific. Her husband Benjamin was in the
sealing trade but was a keen explorer, and his adventurous spirit led him – and his wife – into situations
normally well outside the world of the Hen Frigate.

Curiously, Benjamin also wrote an account of this voyage, but since he was described by a contemporary as 'the greatest liar in the Pacific', his wife's may be a better record of what actually happened, even when dealing with such dramatic incidents as a murderous attack by cannibal islanders. Her account certainly enjoyed larger sales. Apart from the descriptions of exotic places, much of the interest in this book is the traditional, centuries-old world of the sailor as seen through the eyes of a thoughtful and well-educated woman. As such it heads a long line of 'improving' books aimed at ameliorating the seaman's lot.

Born in New York in 1809, the newly wed Abby Morrell insisted on accompanying her husband on a sealing voyage that was to last three years; her brother also went along on this voyage. However, after giving birth to a second son following their return in 1831, Abby remained at home. As a further example of wifely sacrifice, she withheld the publication of her own book until after her husband's was released.

This volume of Seafarers' Voices seems to be unique in three ways. It is the first American account (perhaps the first ever) of a deep-sea voyage left to us by the wife of a merchant captain, who accompanied her husband on the voyage in question. Further, it is possibly the only account where both the husband and the wife have left complementary versions of the same trip, providing a unique insight into a husband and wife team working together – and what each considered important, or came to consider important, on the voyage. Finally, many years before Samuel Plimsoll (1834-1898), the 'seaman's friend', made his pleas for the amelioration of the lot of the common sailor in books such as *Our Seamen* (1873), Abby Morrell makes impassioned but reasoned arguments for better conditions and educational opportunities to be made available to the men before the mast, a call that has still not even today been addressed by many of the world's biggest shipping lines, concerns, and consortiums.

Abby Morrell was born Abby Jane Wood in 1809, the daughter of Captain John Wood, who died at New Orleans in 1811 while master of the ship *Indian Hunter*, a man, we are told, who was judged by his contemporaries as being of 'great integrity'. On his death, Abby Wood Morrell's mother placed their property in the hands of a person who 'by intention or mismanagement lost – or retained – the whole of it'. Matters were rescued when her mother was consoled both by religion and by remarriage, in 1814, to a Mr Burritt Keeler. This stepfather Abby Morrell came to love and feel for 'as much as if he were naturally responsible for my existence and care'. She adds that she had a 'plain and regular education'; and that one of her greatest enjoyments was attending St Paul's Trinity Church, New York.

Early in the year 1824, when she was fifteen, her

cousin, Captain Benjamin Morrell (1795-1831), whom she had not seen since she was five, returned from one of his Pacific voyages, travels that had rendered him both famous and infamous, the latter stemming from his remarks and writings concerning the topography of the Southern Ocean and its land masses, and how far south he had managed to penetrate, what he found there, and how long it took to make these discoveries. Although these observations gained him the title of 'the liar of the Pacific', and he has further been accused of plagiarising the accounts of others, some historians have been more supportive, asserting that his tendency to boastfulness should not diminish his genuine achievements.[2]

Abby Wood married Benjamin Morrell on 29 June 1824. Morrell had been married before; his first wife and their two children had died between 1822 and 1824 whilst he was at sea. A short time after this second marriage, according to Abby's account, Benjamin Morrell informed his wife that he would be leaving on a voyage expected to last about two years, and three weeks later he did so.

Morrell returned on 9 May 1826, two months short of two years, before making a number of short European voyages, during which time a son had been born to the couple. Then in June 1828 Morrell sailed again for the South Seas, this time the separation being eleven months. On his return, his wife determined 'that if he ever went to sea again, I would accompany him.' On hearing new plans for another trading voyage to the Pacific, she now ventured 'to mention my accompanying him.' At first he apparently would not hear of it; but 'when I insisted (as far as affectionate obedience could insist) he at last reluctantly yielded and put the best side outwards.'

Although 'voyaging under these circumstances [might] seem a most remarkable challenge', as Joan Druett points out in her history of those wives of merchant captains who went to sea, Abby Morrell was only one amongst 'a great multitude of women who took up the same strange existence in the blue-water trade', yet astonishingly most of them were, like Abby, 'ordinary, conservative, middle-class women', and 'not rebels or adventurers'[3], even if their husbands could be described as such.

On 2 September 1829, Captain and Mrs Morrell, with twenty-three sailors (one of whom was Mrs Morrell's brother) embarked on the schooner *Antarctic* for the South Pacific, via the Cape of Good Hope. Once there, their aim was to try for a cargo of seal, bêche-de-mer (sea cucumbers), and whatever else might be available to render a profitable voyage.

Once out of sight of New York, it seemed at first that the voyage had been a mistake: Mrs Morrell became anxious for the welfare of her young son who had been left with her mother, and she immediately fell prey to seasickness, telling us that while the Stoics could sustain having their flesh torn by red-hot pincers, 'even the most famed of that sect would look a little pale in a fit of seasickness.'[4] However, Abby Morrell eventually gained her sea legs, and perhaps also became reconciled to her absence from her son, as the account only mentions him again briefly before they are reunited at the end of the voyage.

The ship eventually made Boa Vista, Cape Verde Isles, where Mrs Morrell was relieved once more to see people, having had only the *Antarctic*'s sailors for company for 'the last thirty-three days. Days, in retrospect, that appeared to me nearly as long as my life had been.' The only woman on the ship, and with no specified role on board, time must have hung heavy on her hands on many occasions. But once on board – what was her purpose? She could not navigate; the work of the ship was complex and extremely professional, and needed a great deal of physical stamina – stamina built up over years of unceasing labour. As Druett points out, this difficulty was not particular to Abby Morrell; women at this time 'were expected to be busy and productive' but at sea 'her only real job was to keep the captain company and look after his children, oversee the steward's work in the pantry, entertain the passengers if there were any, and otherwise sit with folded hands.'[5] She would be reduced to being an observer and now, at the Cape Verde Isles, probably realised this. Her account of the voyage is based on the journal she kept on board; this presumably is the thorough account that it is because of the hours she had to spend on writing it. As she tells us, 'passengers surely have leisure when officers have no spare time, the inspiration coming, generally, from the pure air, which after all may be the best inspiring agent in nature'. Perhaps also the long days which needed to be filled, particularly when the ship was becalmed, also inspired her comments on the importance of a copious and well-stocked library on board, for 'in such a situation the nights are restless, the days endless. All that memory can furnish, books can supply, or conversation can offer, is nothing.'

Mrs Morrell probably saw herself, even this early in the voyage, as being there as a commentator on what was to be found ashore in the various ports they would visit. Her account is wide-ranging, with descriptions of ocean and bird life, the geography and history of the places to which they voyaged, not to mention the strange and foreign peoples whom they encountered – her memoir takes the reader right back to the early nineteenth century world of the southern oceans, a world of explorers and missionaries, of 'cannibals' and 'savages'. Although some of her views make uncomfortable reading nowadays, as in her dismissal of 'Hottentots' as 'abject wretches', and her prejudices are typical of her time, she also demonstrates a humanity and desire for amelioration in the condition of the sailors with whom she travelled, and for the education of the peoples with whom she came into contact.

We hear about maritime customs and superstitions: as the *Antarctic* reaches the equator she tells us about the 'crossing the line' ceremony, where 'Neptune' boards the ship, an event which she describes with amused tolerance; she also presents us with the moving spectacle of burial at sea. Other more irrational superstitions such as the legend of the Flying Dutchman she dissects with scientific precision, keen to detail rational explanations for such phenomena.

That this voyage was full of potential danger and one from which a number of sailors did not return alive is made clear, although Abby Morrell's matter-of-fact narrative tone does not sensationalise or exaggerate the perils. She was taken ill with an 'intermittent fever', which then spread to many of the crew, until 'in five or six days, one half were prostrate', and her husband was left trying to run the ship short-handed, not sleeping 'two hours out of twenty-four.' After two crew members died, Mrs Morrell began to think this would be her own fate, feeling horror at the thought that she herself might suffer the fate of being consigned to the waters of the oceans for an eternity.

Benjamin Morrell has left a graphic account of the state of his wife's mind at this time, perhaps worth quoting at length as it provides an insight into their relationship and the way they responded to each other, as well as illuminating the differences between her and her husband's style as a journal writer:

Nov 9th – On Monday, 9 November, I was happy to perceive that the fever had left Mr Scott and two of the seamen, affording reasonable hopes of their ultimate recovery. The rest still remaining in a critical, if not hopeless, situation. . . . My wife sent for and told me that she would no longer conceal from me the fact that her hours were numbered . . . feeling she could not survive another day. She therefore . . . charged me with some messages for her mother, father, brothers, sisters, and our dear little boy – soon to be a motherless orphan. She wished me to cut off some of her hair, and give each of them a lock; with an injunction to preserve it for the sake of one who had loved them, and prayed for their happiness day and night.

'Tell my dear mother not to weep for me,' said she; 'for I shall die happy, and expect to meet her in heaven. Tell my brothers and sisters to be kind to their mother, and to be kind to our dear little boy, and early initiate him in the path of virtue, which alone leads to happiness. I need not ask you, Benjamin, to be kind to your son, the pledge of our mutual loves; but I pray you to be so to my afflicted mother, and all the family. Do not fail to bring up our dear boy in the fear of the Lord. Have a locket made of my hair, and tell little William that he must always wear it about his neck; that when he looks at it, he may be reminded that he once had a fond and doting mother, who blessed him with her dying breath; and teach him to pray that he may meet her in heaven.' After a little pause, she continued: 'There is only one thing, Benjamin, that makes me feel unpleasant; and that is, the idea of my body being thrown overboard and becoming food for sharks.'

As soon as I could command my voice, I assured her, in the most solemn manner, that if her dear spirit was called hence by her Saviour, her mortal covering . . . should be carefully and sacredly preserved, until it could be decently deposited in consecrated ground; or . . . until my return to New York. She thanked me sweetly for this, and said if her body could only be kept from the monsters of the deep, she cared not where it was buried. I repeated my promise, which acted like a charm on her drooping spirits, and wonderfully revived her languishing frame. At her own earnest request, I now left her, to look to the sick officers and seamen, and administer such medicines and refreshments as their circumstances required.[6]

Following Abby Morrell's partial recovery, the *Antarctic* rounded the Cape of Good Hope and called at Desolation Island (Kerguelen Island), a volcanic terrain but which supported a variety of sea life, as well as cabbages with very high concentrations of vitamin C, much sought after by whalers and sailors in the nineteenth century as an anti-scorbutic.

Here came the first commercial disappointment of the voyage. Expecting to take many seal, Benjamin Morrell wrote that 'We therefore stood alongshore . . . under easy sail, examining the islets and coast as we went for fur-seal, but found none. On the different beaches, however, we saw about a thousand sea elephants.' Although the tone of Abby Morrell's account is one of interested onlooker, eager to impart the knowledge gained on such a venture for the edification of her readers, such voyages were not merely exploratory or speculative tours – the prime purpose was commercial, and it was essential for Morrell to be able to turn a profit, covering the costs of his crew and the necessary supplies and defensive armaments.

The *Antarctic* had by then been out almost four months and now headed towards the Auckland islands. Although uninhabited nowadays, at that time Auckland Island seems to have had some sort of supply base, as Mrs Morrell tells us that the crew went onshore to buy provisions, while she was 'assisted on deck' by her husband and brother. Gazing around, weak as she was, she 'felt new life in the ecstasy of the moment, as the very flowers seemed to open to receive me. While there came the sweet warblings of ten thousand beautiful birds within fifty yards of the *Antarctic*'s stern', noting that, 'the animals here . . . have little fear having seldom heard the murderous gun of the sportsman' and 'good fish can be had at all times.'

The schooner also visited the Bay of Islands, a well-known thriving community and missionary base, and together with some English captains, the Morrells called on the missionaries. Abby Morrell clearly enjoyed such opportunities for socialisation and contact with other women, and the company must have offered a welcome relief from that of the crew on board, from whom, as wife of the captain, and a 'lady', she must necessarily have kept a social distance. Her detachment from the business of sailing the ship is indicated in Benjamin's journal of the same voyage. They almost ran aground on one reef and we gain an insight into the ongoing relationship between husband and wife at a time when, according to him, he was trying desperately to save the ship:

> At the very crisis of our fate, my wife came on deck and asked me if I would have my hat! Happily for her, she knew not that we were all tottering on the verge of destruction's precipice. It was the tender officiousness of an affectionate, devoted wife, but at such a crisis inconceivably *mal-apropos*. My reply was not short, and *not* sweet: 'Go below instantly, my dear, or I shall be compelled to have you taken from my presence by force.'[7]

At Manila the *Antarctic* fitted out for the Fiji Islands to search for a cargo of bêche-de-mer. Bêche-de-mer, or sea cucumber, is a sea creature, a Holothurian, and also a food. Considered a great delicacy in Chinese and southeast Asian cultures, they are thought to bestow good health generally, and sexual health specifically. As Captain Morrell puts it, 'The Chinese . . . believing that it wonderfully . . . renews the exhausted vigour of the immoderate voluptuary'[8], perhaps due to a doctrine of signatures, because the bêche-de-mer itself physically resembles a phallus, whilst its defence mechanism resembles human copulation, as it stiffens and squirts a jet of water at any agitator. Bêches-de-mer were traditionally harvested by hand from shallow seabeds by indigenous labour working from small watercraft. In Morrell's day, they were dried in 'bêche-de-mer houses' for preservation purposes, to be later rehydrated by boiling and soaking in water. Today they are mainly used in Chinese cuisine: soups and stews.

At this point the focus of the two Morrell accounts diverges, when Mrs Morrell was forced to remain behind in Manila while her husband departed on the *Antarctic*. The Morrells had become acquainted with the American consul at Manila and Mrs Morrell initially found his attentions towards her 'courteous and friendly – and respectful', but then came the news that the Spanish government were opposed to Mrs Morrell accompanying her husband and that she should remain in Manila. She was puzzled but 'the next time I saw the consul all became plain as day – though I did not tell my husband, for fear of the consequences from his quick sense of injury, while my youth and ignorance made me wonder if I had not put a wrong construction upon the consul's demeanour.' On the contrary, it appeared that she had put exactly the right construction on the consul's demeanour, but nonetheless they were forced to agree to her staying behind, due to threats to impound the *Antarctic* or to take it by force, and particularly after Morrell's attempt to smuggle her aboard was discovered by the consul. Knowing that Morrell's immediate future prospects rested, to a large extent, on the commercial results of his voyage, she eventually stayed in Manila for nearly three months under the protection of three sea captains, friends of Morrell, his business being 'to procure a cargo of bêche-de-mer, tortoiseshell, pearls, pearl-shell, or any other valuables which might be to the profit of the owners'[9], and certainly not to jeopardise the voyage itself.

Abby Morrell tells us that while she was in Manila the *Antarctic* found six islands surrounded by a reef with plenty of bêche-de-mer, but thereafter matters did not go well. The inhabitants not only stole tools and equipment, but also attacked the crew, killing fourteen of the sailors, and wounding another four including her brother. That is the account left by Mrs Morrell – but what of Captain Morrell's journal, the *Four Voyages*? In this, although there is a detailed account of the events leading up to the first trip to Massacre Island, interestingly enough, there is no mention anywhere of the American consul. What we find, at Massacre Island and elsewhere, are accounts of the female inhabitants of the Pacific islands, the young women of these islands seeming to exert a fascination on seamen of all ranks:

> These girls were about sixteen or seventeen, with eyes like the gazelle's, teeth like ivory, and the most delicately formed features I have ever met with. In stature they were about five feet, with small hands, feet, and head, long black hair, and eyes sparkling like jet beads swimming in liquid enamel! Small plump cheeks, with chin to match; and lips of just the proper thickness for affection's kiss. Their necks were small, and I believe that I could have spanned their naked waists with both my hands. Their limbs beautifully proportioned; as were their busts. Bewitching portraits to which I will only add their shade – a light copper colour.[10]

Back in the Philippines, with seventy additional men, sixty-six being natives of Manila, both the Morrells now returned to Massacre Island, 'notwithstanding every effort against us by the consul. But the tooth of the serpent was broken as Messrs Cannell and Gellis advanced my husband all that was required to fit out the ship', and on 1 July 1830, they sailed with a crew of eighty-five men. At this point Abby Morrell offers the reader an interesting comment on the tension inherent in the concept of 'civilisation' as opposed to 'savagery' when she says of her crew 'fifty-five of them as savage and potentially dangerous as those we were about to encounter. Even so, I entered my cabin with a light step – not fearing savage men half so much as a civilised brute [ie, the consul].'

The *Antarctic* called at many islands, some of which Captain Morrell named for friends and some other acquaintances he admired, although most of these names have now been consigned to history. On one island they bought ambergris[11], and 'on 26 November 1830, we discovered islands from which we now took two natives, whom my husband named Sunday and Monday', although the taking of these indigenous people back to America is presented as an opportunity for their self-improvement rather than as an abduction.

In January 1831 the schooner began its voyage back to New York, Mrs Morrell leaving us with her final thoughts on Manila and a graphic account of an earthquake she experienced there. On sailing, it was found that the ship was overladen, and they put in to Singapore where once again we are given an interesting and well-observed account of early nineteenth-century life in what was to become a significant outpost of empire.

Off Mauritius, Abby Morrell made only the second demand of her husband we ever hear about, when she asked him to put in there as she wished to see the grave of Harriet Newell (1793–1812), a would-be missionary to India who was born in Massachusetts, and who died and was buried on Mauritius after her embryonic mission was driven from Calcutta by the East India Company.

Newell (née Atwood) probably had an influential effect
on the young Abby Jane Wood which has never, as yet,
been considered. Newell was 'naturally cheerful and
unreserved; possessed a lively imagination and great
sensibility; and . . . a taste for reading. . . . She
manifested no peculiar and lasting seriousness before the
year 1806 . . . when, at the Academy in Bradford . . . she
first became the subject of those deep religious impressions, which laid the foundation of her Christian life.'[12]
Harriet Atwood married the Rev Samuel Newell in
February 1812, and, with another couple, they went to
preach in India and Burma. After being expelled from
India they went on to Mauritius, where Newell died on
30 November 1812, having given birth to a child who
died after five days. Her memoirs were published
posthumously in the latter part of 1812, the year she died,
going into a number of editions.

Abby Wood would have had open access to these
Memoirs from her own childhood. Comparing the two
books, Newell's *Memoirs* and Abby Morrell's *Narrative*,
there are certain stylistic turns and similarities of
content worth noting, although both are characteristic
of early nineteenth-century evangelical Christian
writing.

Here is Newell:

> We have had the Bible in our hands from our
> childhood; we are instructed regularly from this

precious volume, every Sabbath . . . we enjoy the
stated ordinances of the gospel. But the dear Heathen
have no such privileges. They are destitute of Bibles,
Sabbaths, and churches. The inhabitants of
Hindustan . . . submit to the most cruel tortures
imaginable. Widows consent to be burned with their
deceased husbands; parents sacrifice their infant
offspring to appease the anger of their idol gods . . .
But this dreadful superstition vanishes before the
benignant rays of the gospel, as the morning dew
before the rising sun.[13]

Morrell writes:

If there ever was a book which could be called an
awakener of our own thoughts, it is that which
furnishes so many thoughts for us, the Bible. I have
read it where Christianity was professed, followed,
and held the highest claims to attention; I have read
it where superstition abounds, and where infidelity,
pagan infidelity, darkened the whole land: it was the
same heaven-illumined page everywhere; but if ever
peculiar glory rested on it, it was when we were near
those who had never received its glad tidings, and
who never knew the true God.

As can be seen from the above extracts, both women
regarded missionary work as one of the highest callings,
one whose claimed motives for exploration of distant
lands and engagement with the indigenous populations

were altruistic rather than appropriative, unlike traders
and state-backed explorers, whose depredations rever-
berate to the present day, so making Morrell's account
of continuing historical interest.

In the latter part of this three-year voyage, the
Antarctic stopped off at St Helena, Cadiz and Bordeaux
– we hear more about history and politics and culture as
seen through the eyes of Abby Morrell, and gain insights
into contemporary life in these places. On the last leg of
the journey, as Abby Morrell says, 'the distance seemed
a mere trifle, three thousand miles, and that across the
Atlantic; my own ocean, which I did not think now
would be deceitful, since I had braved so many dangers
in the southern Pacific.' Such has been the vividness of
the account that the reader, too, has been taken to the
South Seas and back.

By the time that the *Antarctic* arrived back in New
York in August 1831, and Mrs Morrell was greeted by
her family, she found that her stepfather and one of her
aunts had died, but her mother and her son were well,
and 'nine days after my return I was the happy mother
of another fine son. Perhaps his mother's *Journal* may
in some future day be read by him; and perhaps he may
be stimulated to put some of her plans in train.'

We have read the story of a hardy and a courageous
woman who demonstrates a basic bravery in being
always ready to accept and face what came along
without too much consideration of self. The writing in

both her account and that of her husband (whether ghostwritten or not) seems a spirited mixture of both *Grand Guignol* and Gilbert and Sullivan – but also shot through with an unblinking view of the sort of world in which early Pacific traders found themselves, when torture, death, and the cooking pot seemed to lurk within every coral reef.

The character of Benjamin Morrell is largely outside the remit of this work. What can be said of Abby Morrell is that in 1829 she went boldly where only a minority of women ventured, and is one of the first to leave an accessible account, and to have this account published. Because there was little or nothing to occupy her on board, her thoughts and observations were of seaports and their peoples, flora and fauna; speculations on the deep and its inhabitants; the mysteries of the heavens and what lies beneath the waves and, over all, on the God whom she believed unassailably had brought into being all that existed in and beyond her world. She took what was on offer and seems to have dealt with it in honesty, and as best she knew how.

To admire her bravery would always have to be a unanimous decision among the fair-minded; to salute her would always have to be the natural reaction of any person who has made a long, enervating, deep-sea voyage.

Captain's Wife

Preface

IN FIRST TAKING up my pen, I intended nothing more than a plain narrative of the events of my voyage in the schooner, *Antarctic*. But as I proceeded, I felt a desire to address a subject which became of greater interest to me – a plea for an amelioration of the lot of the American seaman. It may be thought strange that a woman should address this subject. Perhaps, though, being a woman, I am better qualified to offer a few suggestions, rather than any of those engaged in the navy or merchant service, who might be suspected of wishing to gain promotion or employment.

And while I tremble to think I am about to put my thoughts before the general public, perhaps they will listen to me kindly. For while it is seldom that a female can know anything of these matters, I had an opportunity of becoming acquainted with them during the years 1829, '30, '31, and should be proud to try to be a humble instrument in improving the conditions, and moral and intellectual standards of our American seamen, a race which ever has and ever will add to the prosperity and glory of our country, and the reformation of whose habits requires no argument to prove how much it would benefit commerce.

AJM
New York, January 1833

1. I persuade my husband to allow me to accompany him on his voyage. We leave New York, July 1829, for the southern Pacific Ocean. We bury one of our men dead from intemperance. Cape Verde Islands. Crossing the equator I meet King Neptune. A severe fever visits the ship and my life is feared for. Tristan da Cunha and the Island of Desolation.

MY MAIDEN NAME was Abby Jane Wood, and I was born on 17 February 1809 in the city of New York. My father was Capt John Wood, who died at New Orleans on 14 November 1811 while master of the ship, *Indian Hunter*. And although I was so young that I could not judge of his virtues, it has been a source of happiness to me ever since that he is always spoken of by his contemporaries as a man of great integrity.

At his death, my mother placed our property in the hands of a person who by intention or mismanagement lost – or retained – the whole of it, a grievous affliction for her as she was now left with a family of helpless children. The belief that she was vilely robbed at first preyed upon her mind, but the consolations of religion lifted her above her troubles, and in 1814 she married Mr Burritt Keeler, a gentleman of a kind and generous disposition to whom I feel as much as if he were naturally responsible for me, my existence and care.

My childhood passed as that of other children, bringing both pleasures and pains, while my early education was plain and regular in a respectable New York school. One of my greatest enjoyments was derived from Sunday's attendance at St Paul's Trinity Church, which left me precepts I later often called upon while floating upon the vast ocean.

Early in the year 1824 when I was fifteen, my cousin Capt Benjamin Morrell, whom I had not seen since I was five, returned from a long voyage to the Pacific Ocean. At our first interview I felt a friendship for him I had never felt for anyone before. His personal appearance, gentlemanly manners, and humane disposition, as well as his adventures, had an immediate effect on me and after constantly visiting for several weeks, he offered his hand. The match being acceptable to my parents, we were married on 29 June 1824. A short time later he informed me that he was to sail on a two years' voyage. Although I knew when I married him I was to be the wife of a seafaring man it was impossible for me as a fifteen-year-old bride to realise the distress of separation. Barely three weeks had passed when on

18 July his voyage began, and for many nights my dreams were only of him being tossed by storms, engulfed in the deep, or wrecked on desolate isles subjected to the violence of savages. He has good sailors with him, said my friends, but good sailors are not the same as a good wife, I thought. In this manner passed my nights and days, until he returned on 9 May 1826, two months short of two years, when my happiness was again complete.

After several European voyages during which we had a son who bore a striking resemblance to his father, in June 1828 my husband sailed again for the South Seas. This separation was such that I determined that if he ever went to sea again, I would accompany him. He returned on 14 July 1829, and was planning another voyage to the Pacific when I now ventured to mention my accompanying him. At first he would not hear of it, but when I insisted (as far as affectionate obedience could insist) he at last reluctantly yielded, and once agreed he put the best side outwards.

On 2 September 1829 ourselves and twenty-three good sailors (one of whom was a brother of mine) embarked on the schooner *Antarctic*. A fine breeze soon wafted us from the shores of my native country, but as we distanced ourselves from the land I began to feel anxious for the welfare of my boy, whom I had left with my mother. I knew he was in good hands, but those hands were not mine and I now learned that nothing will satisfy a mother in regard to her offspring but her own care.

I began to grow seasick, a sensation that cannot be described, but which prostrates sense, fortitude, feelings, and reduces an adult to the baby. I became quite exhausted but, as I had insisted on making the voyage, did not suffer myself to complain. My husband did everything in his power to make me comfortable, but all to no avail. I would walk until I felt faint, or perhaps take up a book. But in a few moments the lines would swim before my eyes, and a tale of the deepest interest would affect me no more than the dullest story ever told. I have read of Stoics showing no emotion, wearing a smile while their flesh was torn with hot pincers, but believe even the most famed of that sect would look a little pale in a fit of seasickness.

Eventually it ameliorated, and I was able to come out on deck and begin to pay attention. All was new to me, the management of the ship, the discipline of the sailors, etc, who were all so respectful towards my husband and myself, and so gentle towards each other, that one would have thought them a band of brothers.

And then the ocean: a magnificent boundless expanse with huge whales tumbling around our vessel, not regarding her any more than an eggshell floating by. Dolphins, too, were seen in great number, often pursuing flying-fish, who to avoid their pursuers would take to the air for the space of half a minute or more, some weighing nearly half a pound, then landing on deck.

On 29 September one of the crew, Francis Patterson, died after a very severe illness brought on by drink. My husband had shipped his crew upon condition that they should abstain from all spirits, unless served as medicine, and was the first captain, I believe, to ever do so for so long a voyage. Patterson had reached the age of sixty-three, but had too long used liquor to live many more years, whether he abstained or not. A fine old sailor with only a single failing, but a great one. At four o'clock in the afternoon his funeral took place. I had supposed that the body would be thrown overboard without much ceremony, but instead the service was the most solemn I ever witnessed. The body was laid out with great decency, then enveloped in a hammock and sewed up with about fifty pounds of stones secured to the feet. The corpse was then extended upon a plank on the rail at the starboard gangway, and all hands called to join in prayers, the faces of the hardy crew now wet with tears. The ship's colours were set at half-mast, and the topsails and topgallant sails settled on the cap. Prayers being over, a gun was fired from the bows, and the body launched into the ocean. At home I had seen and heard the first shovelfuls of earth thrown upon a coffin, but that was not so bad as this plunge into the deep. In a graveyard a friend might visit, might erect an inscribed stone. But here, no mortal would ever tell where he was laid! I was awakened from this reverie by the shrill pipe of the boatswain calling all hands back to duty. In an instant, the sails were set and we were gliding onward, each seaman looking as if he felt he had 'done his duty'.

The mate wrote this sentimental epitaph in the logbook: 'Buried Francis Patterson this day, latitude 16° 35' north, longitude 26° 2' west from Greenwich. He died yesterday. Weather fair, winds light.'

These winds continued until 4 October, when a sailor announced land on our starboard bow. My husband went up the mast, I watching his ascension without emotion, although a month before I should have gone into fits. The land was St Nicholas, Cape Verde Islands. The next day we saw Boa Vista, and in the afternoon came to anchor in the harbour about two miles from the town, with a refreshing offshore breeze. It was very pleasant to again see land, shipping, churches, etc, and especially people, having seen only our sailors for the last thirty-three days, days in retrospect that appeared to me nearly as long as my life had been.

Early next morning we received a visit from the health officer, then at 10am my husband and myself went ashore to meet the governor. He, with his amiable family and friends, received us with great kindness. Kind attentions are at all times pleasant, but away from home they are delightful indeed. Our stay was short, but I shall long remember that accomplished family who even attended us to the boat, their servants bearing such presents as they felt we would want on our voyage. We ladies embraced, and left each other with tears. There is something in these transient attachments, I feel, which shows that we are all born to do each other good, notwithstanding all the evil in the world.

We were soon out of sight. Our bark was moving at eight or nine miles an hour, but I stood silent. There is something soothing in rapidity of motion when minds have been agitated by thoughts and feelings.

Early next morning we made St Jago, anchoring in the harbour. The bottom, I noticed, was beautiful white sand. The flag of the American consul, Mr Merrill, was flying about a mile and a half distant. We went on shore and were again very kindly received. Here I had pointed out to me the ruins of a castle, said to be that of the famous Blue Beard, as this island and those in the neighbourhood were the rendezvous of the buccaneers of America, who, after their depredations, used these places for security. As this island abounds in vegetables, we took in a good stock, and filled our casks with pure water.

We now made the best of our way towards the equator accompanied by frequent falls of rain, and quick and heavy thunder and lightning, flash following flash until the heavens seemed one continuous blaze. On 23 October 1829 we crossed the Line, in longitude 22° 10' W. About 4pm I witnessed a visit from Neptune who, with great good nature, shaved a few of the green hands who had never before crossed the equator, and all made merry without one drop of liquor. And although he did not pretend to have any power over a female sailor who had never crossed the equator, I propitiated him with a few small presents. These things are pleasant enough to pass away an hour, and I began to realise that the art of managing sailors consists in keeping them temperate, industrious, clean, and cheerful. They are always obedient when healthy and comfortable.

We had now got into the southeast trade winds, and the weather being pleasant, my husband began to exercise the crew in the management of the big guns, and the use of small arms. 'Yankee Doodle', which was played when the men had closed their exercises, always sounded very pleasant in my ears.

On 20 October, I was taken sick with an intermittent fever, as were eleven of the crew, and some officers. The disease advanced so rapidly that in five or six days nearly one half of all on board were prostrate, my husband being so constantly employed in attending to the vessel and the sick, that I believe he did not sleep two hours out of twenty-four. My brother now proved of great assistance to my husband, as well as being a great comfort to me.

On 2 November it was a bad day for we buried Samuel Gerry, and now my husband began to believe that nearly all his crew would die of fever, especially as the next day Daniel Spinney died. I, too, began to think that it was my fate to also be buried at sea, pendent in mid ocean being devoured by sharks, or spending whole ages rising and sinking in a world of waters.

At last the fever left us, when I found myself drawn up like a cripple, but by the kind attention of my husband I began to recover, although I was a long time in getting into an erect position. In so short a time will sickness bring down the firmest constitution.

My husband determined on touching at Tristan da Cunha for the purpose of getting fresh provisions for the sick, and on 15 November 1829 we sent a boat ashore on the north side of the island, the only part inhabited. Carried on deck to catch the mild breeze I saw about seven or eight men, as many women, and about twenty children gathered together with their goats and hogs. A variety of beautiful birds were also to be seen. In fact, the whole shore teemed with animated nature: shellfish, seal, sea elephants, and wildfowl, excellent fish for the table, especially a kind of perch. Also right whales, particularly the females, playing with their young round the shores, not daring to trust their progeny to the wide and boisterous ocean until they have gained strength. Affection seems not confined to our breathing atmosphere, but to life everywhere. That such monsters should feel so seems strange, but would it not be stranger if such a body be made without affections?

On the north-northwest side of this island is a bay
open to the north wind. This beach is of black sand, and
extremely beautiful, and there are two or three
sparkling cataracts upon the steeps from which
excellent water is taken without difficulty. The land is
formed of high ridges and deep chasms, and is probably
of volcanic origin. The highlands are covered with
forests, bearing the appearance of yew trees. A great
variety of plants grow, proving the soil fit for almost any
kind of cultivation. It is free from reptiles and wild
beasts, and seems only to have come up from the ocean
for the benefit of man. Tristan da Cunha has two
neighbouring islands, Inaccessible Island and Nightin-
gale Island.

After getting a good store of hogs, sheep, fowls and
vegetables, we sailed. For a few days we had pleasant
weather, then a gale struck – the first since New York.
It was tremendous, and I was several times violently
thrown out of my berth, and every moment I expected
the ship to sink. It finally abated on 1 December. We
continued our course round the Cape of Good Hope for
the Island of Desolation (49° 15' S/69° 35' E) with
strong winds, and now and then storms of hail and
snow. On 5 December we were again cheered by 'Land
ahead!', and soon entered the harbour discovered by
Capt James Cook in 1776. No place in either hemisphere
affords a better field for a naturalist than this. The
seabirds, including several kinds of albatrosses, are so

numerous and thick, they get in each other's way. Seals and sea elephants were once numerous here also.

From this romantic place we sailed for Lord Auckland's group (50° 42' S/166° 5' E). I now began to regain my appetite, and to attend once more to what was happening around me. I saw but little of my husband, as the weather was boisterous, and his officers still so weak he spent most of his time on the deck. If his gentleness and benevolence had initially won my heart, his bravery now excited my admiration and pride; he was so capable of taking care of others, the sailors, for their part, being full of confidence towards one who had knelt at all the beds of the sick and dying, as well as at mine – and always with energy, hope, and fortitude. This latter was much needed on our passage to Auckland's group, as we had no galley fire with the waves sweeping over us, while our sails were constantly splitting and our spars falling. However, on 29 December 1829 we reached this group, and dropped anchor at eleven in the morning.

2. Lord Auckland's Group. The Bay of Islands, New Zealand. Whale ships. A missionary establishment. Visit to the king and queen. Strong's Island. Appearance of the natives. Discovery of several islands. We reach Manila where I am plagued by the American consul. My husband sails without me to Massacre Isle for bêche-de-mer. His misfortunes when attacked by cannibals.

ONCE AT ANCHOR the crew went onshore to buy provisions, while I was assisted on deck by my husband and brother. Weak as I was, I felt new life in the ecstasy of the moment, as the very flowers seemed to open to receive me, while there came the sweet warblings of ten thousand beautiful birds among forest trees which grew within fifty yards of the *Antarctic*'s stern. These birds are large paroquets and wood-pigeons, and a great variety of small birds. Among the latter there is a green bird, about the size of a robin, whose melody and notes are so varied, that one might imagine himself regaled by a hundred different songsters at once. The animals here are mostly strangers to man and have little fear, having seldom heard the murderous gun of the sportsman. The fish are good, and can be had at all times. As well as fish, the albatross and aquatic birds abound in the sea.

The hills, at the bases of which are set small caves, begin to rise almost from the water's edge with deep valleys between them. The forests here are very luxuriant, covered with unknown plants; one in parti-cular is a species of flax that bears a yellow flower. The threads in its heart are silky, and in the opinion of my husband it could be raised in our southern states to supersede both flax and hemp. The season here at this time (December) answers to our July, though the thermometer here does not rise above 55° at noon.

On 4 January 1830 we sailed in fine order as if on a new voyage, and on the 6th saw the south cape of New Zealand. The boats were sent off to examine the shore, but found no seal, the obtaining of whose fur being one object of the voyage. The boats now investigated the shores of Night Island, and on 12 January we had a visit from some natives, who came off in a war canoe containing about fifty men, two of whom were principal chiefs, whimsically tattooed, and their bodies stained with red or blue.

The major occupation of these people seems to be war. They carry about with them a greater variety of weapons than most savages, their dexterity with which is considered surprising throughout the southern hemisphere. Their looks are bold and fierce, they have much martial dignity, delight in the war song, and carry their fury to the greatest excess. They are, as near as I could learn, cannibals. And when prisoners are taken, they frequently cut from them, while alive, pieces of flesh which they then masticate to show fiendish joy at their success. They believe that the spirit of him thus devoured suffers everlasting punishment in the world of spirits for allowing himself to be overthrown. Their affections are strong, and in mourning their own dead they cut themselves in frenzy and tear their flesh, while uttering the most piercing cries. Polygamy is allowed, a chief having as many wives as he wishes to maintain. The females generally unite young, many becoming mothers at the age of twelve or fourteen. Ignorance is the mother of superstition, and their priests keep them in fear. Of course, the love of God is not known where ignorance abounds. They have more curiosity than our North American Indian, for they examined the *Antarctic* with great scrutiny and apparent delight, then took their departure in the most peaceful manner.

On 19 January we saw Cape Briton, and soon after came to anchor in the Bay of Islands, about five miles east of the missionary establishment. Here we found several English whaling ships whose captains treated us with the greatest kindness. I dined on board each in turn, and received every attention that could be paid to a female in a distant country. On 20 January 1830 the English captains, my husband, and myself, went to pay our respects to the missionaries, my heart overflowing to be once more in the embraces of Christian friends.

'Oh! There *is* religion in the world!' said I, when I saw the accomplished females who had left all the comforts and vanities of English society to come to these shores of heathen ignorance. Their labours were incessant, allowing themselves no more than eight hours for repose and meals, with all the rest of the time being devoted to Christianising. The male missionaries work many hours in the field learning the natives' cultivation, plus teaching them to read and write. The wives and daughters, meanwhile, teach the females to sew and to read. The natives are devout and tractable, the influence of the missionaries extremely powerful. A few years ago no ship's crew could land without arms, but now sailors may travel anywhere for a hundred miles around the mission.

When a vessel arrives, the natives flock to it, bringing with them the fruits of their agriculture in great quantities, and at the lowest prices. A quarter of a dollar here will purchase more than could be had for two dollars in New York. Common kitchen-garden vegetables are excellent, apples may be had, and small meats and poultry in abundance. There is little beef at the moment, but soon will be raised as much as will be required. How then could anyone doubt the efficacy of our religion? Here Christianity has been planted where once only darkness and pestilence reigned.

We remained with these good people until about four o'clock in the afternoon, for although they were anxious to have us stay with them while we were on the coast the captains declined, not thinking it proper to sleep away from their vessels.

However, my husband consented that I might stop for one night. This I did, joining in their devotions while thinking that I was joining the prayers of those who had lived in a paradise – though in primitive innocence. But now inflexible duty would not suffer my husband to linger, and I was obliged to take a painful farewell of Mr Davis and his daughters, Mr Williams and his wife and daughters, and some natives, all of whom prayed for my temporal and eternal happiness, sang a hymn that went to my soul, then accompanied me to the beach with tears, embraces, and kisses. On boarding the *Antarctic* I was received by my brother and our brave tars with three hearty cheers, echoed by the crews of all the English ships and a thousand native voices.

However, the wind now blowing onshore, we could not sail as expected. The natives, seeing this, brought an invitation from their king and queen. This was 23 January 1830. The boats of the *Antarctic* were prepared, as were those of other ships, amounting in all to twelve whaleboats. On touching shore again we were met by King Kippy-Kippy. His queen approached, and courteously extended her hand to me. She then waved a fan and seven thousand of her train broke into a song of joyous welcome. They then formed two double parallel lines, the females composing the inner, and the males the outer. The women all bore a green branch in their hands, the heads of the men being ornamented with feathers. As we advanced, the females fell on both knees, the males on one knee. I was set on a sort of chair decorated with feathers of different kinds by six of the principal warriors. These, wearing ornaments of surpassing beauty, now proceeded with great state and solemnity.

Fifty yards from the king's palace, we found the pathway was strewn with beautiful wild flowers. At the palace door elegant mats were spread, holding a superb banquet of the choicest fruits, while young women sang melodious songs and two hundred warriors gave a war dance. The king then made a speech in good English praising the missionaries, saying that before they came the natives had eaten human flesh, but now could sleep without fear of being killed. Night coming on, I informed the queen that I must go back on board, at which she clasped me in her arms, and kissed me several times. I did not consider these honours were paid to me as an individual, but to all females of my own country, and of the English nation. She made me many presents, and I was attended back to the boats with great ceremony. The tars, both English and American, dropped their oars at a signal, and the boats were propelled like dolphins through the water. In a few minutes we reached the *Antarctic*, where we found a great many canoes alongside, loaded with potatoes and hogs – more presents from the king and queen. My final thought was how this once terrifying monarch of fierce warriors was now as courteous as a man brought up in the bosom of polished society thanks to the missionaries.

The next morning, 24 January, we put to sea in a fresh breeze and light rain for Manila. We continued with occasionally thick weather until on 19 February in the morning we saw Strong's Island (lat 5° 58' N/long 162° 55') – about ten leagues in circumference, and of moderate height, the uplands all covered with thick forest, the low grounds with fruit trees. The appearance of the natives here is wild. They have long hair, and light copper-coloured complexions. Their canoes are from ten to fifty feet, and paddled with great dexterity. They have a great partiality for trinkets, red paint, and cutlery. An old iron hoop will purchase a plentiful supply of fruit, a strong proof that they are not often visited by Europeans, as Indians soon grow sagacious in their traffic. It is thought that this island contains sandalwood and other valuables.

We continued our voyage, and on the morning of the 23rd saw seven islands surrounded by a coral reef, not to be found on any of our plentiful charts. These we passed but that same night, breakers were heard ahead, but timely precautions by my husband avoided all difficulties, although the men were much frightened. The morning showed us the coral reef on which we had almost stranded. Inside its circle were a group of islands, four being large and high, and covered with timber and fruit trees. Several canoes were within the reef, filled with men who seemed to wish us to anchor. One of these canoes ventured towards us. The men were large, long-haired, and of a light mulatto colour, warlike in their appearance, but showing no hostility. To these islands my husband gave the name of Bergh's Group, in honour of Edwin Bergh of New York.

We kept on towards Manila and on 5 March arrived at the Straits of St Bernardino, coming to anchor in the evening. In the morning we passed through, and on the evening of 10 March 1830 arrived at Manila (long 121° 0' 9" E/lat 14° 35' N.)

The next morning we were visited by the health officer, and in the afternoon landed. This island, of great interest to the commercial world, was early settled by the Spaniards, who built a walled city for security, narrow at each end and wide in the middle. A fine river runs through it, lending to cleanliness, a rare virtue anywhere. The houses are tastefully built – some being wholly of stone – but all having their first storey of this material. The roofs are flat and most have a piazza, for air and exercise. The streets are broad and airy, the promenades elegant. The inhabitants are about sixteen thousand in number. This is an old country, older than my own, and has had its vicissitudes. But its course has been quiet and colonial, and the Spanish sway has never been interrupted except when it was taken by the British in 1762. It was ransomed at a million sterling, which has never been paid. The inhabitants have now no particular longings for Spain, but speak of it as we Americans do of England, while here all enjoy a freedom perhaps not known in the mother country. But the hope of the Spanish in founding a great eastern empire was never realised, and now never can be. It would not be difficult for a spirited people to conquer the Philippine Islands, but unborn ages will probably pass away before these possessions will become an object to any great maritime power. Yet so jealous still is Spain of her eastern possessions that a large body of troops is kept here as a standing army to repel any attempt to take these territories from her. The government itself, although arbitrary, is seldom oppressive, but there have been times when the Europeans from some assumed apprehension have made general massacres among the Chinese with whom the suburbs of Manila are crowded. These are a skilful people, more industrious than the

Spaniards. It is also said they are honest, comparatively speaking, I suppose.

The soil of the island is fertile and cultivated. Sugar cane, a great staple in their commerce, grows abundantly, while all the usual vegetables are plentiful. To me, born and bred in a country having frost and snow for nearly half the year, it was delightful to experience perpetual verdure, where fruits and flowers hung together by a law of nature and seemed to shadow forth the destiny of man.

The principal food of the poor is fish, of which the waters are full. Indeed, they are so abundant they are used for manure at certain seasons of the year. The fishing canoes of the natives are seen day and night on the waters, each carrying a stern light, which makes a most picturesque appearance. The women on board are equally industrious as the husbands and, however poor, there is no appearance of slatternliness about them – everything in their dress is neat, even if not worth ten cents.

There is but little appearance of business within the city, as most of the merchants live outside the walls. Those who live within seem only to exist to enjoy themselves. Devotions, and amusement, are the duties of the day. The churches are numerous, and of an imposing appearance. It is said there are more convents in Manila than any other city in the world of its size, all said to be under excellent regulation, with their inmates as busy at their devotions, as those of the world at their pleasures. Indeed, with all its parade and ceremony, the Catholic religion can be said to have one singular property – all those who profess it are quite content with it. They seldom disturb themselves with abstruse speculations. There is something within its forms that makes the enlightened as much attached to it as the ignorant. I was born a Protestant, and trust I shall die a Protestant, but hereafter I shall have more charity for all who love religion, whatever their creed.

Females are always the leaders in civilisation and Christianity, and here the Spanish lady is always a high-bred woman, with much chivalry about her. Some have splendid complexions of a bright orange tinge, with fine eyes and beautiful hair, well-turned limbs and a graceful walk. If they had as much application as genius, they would have no superiors in the world. They have an air of grace that marks them from most other females, and I have noticed their walk with admiration. A little of the martial staidness, combined with the elastic tread of the Lady of the Lake. You could say firmness and lightness were never more happily blended than in those females of genteel society who walk the promenades of this city. With them walking is as much of a science and art as playing upon the Spanish guitar, and I wish it was more attended to in my own country. I have heard an anecdote on this subject which has always struck me as containing a wholesome piece of satire. An American female, some years ago, attended by her husband, a naval hero, took a voyage to South America. Of an adventurous spirit, she travelled into the interior mounted on a milk-white horse and being dressed in pure and elegant simplicity, and possessing a splendid form and face, the inhabitants took her for the Madonna, and bowed and fell before her. Then she alighted, when they immediately questioned her divinity – because she had an awkward walk.

The ladies of Manila generally keep a cabinet of beautiful shells, and a large collection of birds of splendid plumage. These shells are often tastefully arranged, and they have a method of keeping the plumage of their birds as beautiful as it was in the groves and in the rays of the sun. Great care is taken to preserve them with such spices as will prevent insects from injuring them.

During a great portion of the year Manila is healthy, but there are seasons during which it is visited by severe sicknesses when cholera carries off thousands. When I was there it was more confined to the country, as in the city they think they have in some measure got the control of the disease. Yet the people do not think much of death, for there is a sort of Asiatic notion of predestination which makes them less attentive to curing or warding off disease than with my own countrymen. But if they are not so anxious to prevent death, they are more attentive to the remains of the dead. The bodies of the Spaniards are buried in the church or convent yards, or under the churches, with every due and solemn form. Sometimes in the country you will see a tombstone, and by its side a large tamarind tree which supplies the place of a weeping willow in the United States, or a yew tree in England. The Indians are, if possible, more attentive to sepultural rites than the Spaniards, for they hold with ancient superstitions that the ghost is restless until the due burial rites are performed.

There are always some drawbacks in every country. Here at times you are dreadfully annoyed by red ants that, like the frogs of Egypt, come up to the kneading troughs, and to the very beds of the sensitive dons. It requires Yankee ingenuity to keep them from devouring you. The mosquitoes, too, are very troublesome, large, sharp-set and poisonous. This insect, I believe, breeds everywhere nature is bountiful, and the soil luxuriant: an enemy impossible to fight, except on the defensive by using smoke and nettings.

I dwell, perhaps, too much on this city, but must be excused, for it was here that I suffered much in my mind, although I found good friends among strangers. I have a painful tale to relate, but one of which it is possible for me to give no more than a faint outline. The cause of our troubles is now dead. But I know no reason why the truth as regards him and his deeds should not be told, if done without bitterness or a spirit of revenge.

Soon after our arrival my husband became acquainted with the American consul, a man of respectable acquirements and of courteous manners. A few days later, Mr Morrell determined to fit out the *Antarctic* for a voyage to the Fiji Islands for the purpose of getting a cargo of tortoiseshell, bêche-de-mer, and other articles, and we all became busy and happy in getting ready for the voyage. At this time the consul's attentions to me were courteous and friendly and, as yet, respectful. I discovered later that already my husband had began to suspect the consul's intentions towards me, although I was not told of this. A few days before we were to sail, my husband told me that the Spanish government were opposed to my going with him to the Fijis, but could give no reason for it. I found this extremely suspicious as I could not suspect my husband of deceiving me. However, the next time I saw the consul all became plain as day, though I did not tell my husband for fear of the consequences from his quick sense of injury, while my youth and ignorance made me wonder if I had not put a wrong construction upon the consul's demeanour.

Instead, I told my husband that painful as our separation might be, if the *Antarctic*'s owners' interest required it, I would remain at Manila if he would provide me with a respectable place in which to reside. This proved to be with an English family named Cannell, of the firm Cannell and Gellis. Now being told by my husband that this worthy family was being vilely aspersed, within and without doors, by the consul, I determined at all hazards to go on the voyage to the Fijis with my husband.

On the day the *Antarctic* was ready for sea my husband had me secretly smuggled on board, so privately done I did not think my persecutor would have found it out, but in this I was deceived.

When my husband came on board, just before sailing, he brought with him for final farewells two American captains, Daggett and Snow of Boston, and an English captain, Harris, from London, and also the second captain of the port, an officer of the customs. Then suddenly the consul was now on the ship. An altercation took place between him and my husband, in which he used every threat he could think of to prevent my sailing, claiming that he had pledged himself to the Spanish government that I should not go in the vessel and it would be ruin to him if he did not redeem his pledge, adding that if I was not put ashore, he would take the *Antarctic* by force. This was an idle threat as we were out of the reach of the fort and gunboats, and had a crew that would have destroyed the consul and his accomplices in an instant. My husband, in what was a death blow to me, at last consented I should go on shore. For an hour after hearing this I was bereft of my senses. But on recovering I found the three captains I have mentioned telling my husband that they would protect me in all events. I shall remember them with gratitude as long as my heart has a pulse to beat.

I was now put in a boat and carried ashore. There being no conveyance ready to take me to Mr Cannell's, I was now obliged to stand on the landing place subject to the gaze of every rude wretch gathered there. And curiosity had collected many! From their appearance, I was fully satisfied that the consul had scattered slanders about me in order that I might feel myself so ruined as to fly to him for protection. But I had made up my mind to die before I would even speak to him, and was at length conveyed to Mr Cannell's mansion to be treated with every possible kindness.

I afterward learned that Mr Morrell came on shore that night, and not finding the Spanish head of the revenue from whom he wished to enquire about my protection then went to a hotel until he could find the man the next morning. Now the American consul, who had been watching my husband's movements, arrived. But so did Snow, Daggett, and Harris, who were standing by, fearing that blood might be spilled.

The consul now said the *Antarctic* was showing false lights, and that my husband and his crew intended mischief to the city. This was hotly denied, but my husband's friends, seeing that desperate events might occur, took him by force and put him on board the *Antarctic*, extracting from him a pledge to proceed to sea, while they giving theirs that I should be shielded. I was under the protection of the Cannells and these three worthy men from 12 April 1830 until the return of the *Antarctic* on 26 June.

My story was soon known to all in Manila. The government became acquainted with it, and immediately disavowed every connection with what was happening, which proved the consul's gross villainy in pretending to act for the government while he was still annoying me with notes I would not answer.

But even though fifteen thousand miles from home, lonely and distressed, I was still more constantly agitated for my husband's safety than for my own. Then, on the seventy-fifth day after his sailing, as I was looking with a glass from my window, I saw my husband's signal at the masthead of an approaching vessel. I communicated this to my friends, who hastened to carry me on board where I was immediately in my husband's arms, but the scene being too much for my enfeebled frame, I became insensible. On coming to, I saw my brother looking pale and emaciated, and that the crew seemed sadly reduced in number. Hardly daring to trust myself, I asked what had become of the men.

My husband detailed how, after leaving Manila, they had discovered several islands. But these not affording the articles he was in search of, continued his voyage until 23 May, when he came to six islands that were surrounded by a reef. Here was plenty of bêche-de-mer. He made up his mind to get a cargo of this, and what tortoiseshell he might procure. He sent a boat's crew onshore, to clear away the brush, and prepare a place to cure the bêche-de-mer. The natives now came off to the vessel, and seemed quiet, although it was evident that they had never seen a white man before, nor did the island bear any trace of having been visited by civilised men. These natives were large and savage-looking, but Mr Morrell was lulled by their harmless actions, and their fondness of visiting the vessel to exchange fruit for trinkets. They, in turn, appeared pleased with the attentions paid them.

The crew were even employed for several days in planting seeds in different parts of the island, where the best soil was found, to produce such things as it was thought would be useful to the natives in the future.

Then the forge and blacksmith's tools were got on shore, but the savages soon stole the greater part of them. My husband, thinking to recover them, took six men, well armed, to the village where the king lived. Here he met two hundred painted warriors, armed with bows and arrows, and eager to fight. On turning, he saw nearly as many more in his rear. It was a critical moment. Seeing that if he did not act in a most dauntless manner death would be inevitable, he threw down his musket and drew his cutlass. Then, taking up a pistol in his right hand, pressed it to king's breast, whilst holding the cutlass above the king's head. The savages had arrowed their bows, but seeing the danger to their king, dropped them to the ground. The king was then conducted, with several of his chiefs, on board the *Antarctic*, and kept until next day, treated with every attention but strictly guarded. On the following morning my husband gave them a good breakfast, loaded them with presents, for which they seemed grateful, and sent them back ashore. He also sent some of the crew ashore to go on with building a house for drying the bêche-de-mer, accompanied by a second group all well armed, plus more presents for those chiefs who had not been on board. All was unavailing for suddenly a general attack came from the woods, in which the *Antarctic*'s crew were soon overthrown. Two who were still in the small boat made their escape out of the reach of the arrows, and picked up three others who had precipitated themselves into the water. On hearing the yells, the whaleboat was sent from the *Antarctic* with another ten men, who with great exertions saved two more. All the rest, fourteen in all, fell victims to savage barbarity! Murdered, mangled, and their corpses thrown upon the beach without the possibility of a Christian burial. Four were wounded – including my brother. The blacksmith's forge and all tools were lost. Now the spirits of the crew broke down, and a sickness came over them that would not yield to the power of medicine – because it arose from moral causes.

In this situation, Capt Morrell made the best of his way back to Manila. His narrative filled my dreams for many nights, and while I dreaded the thought of it, yet I wished I had been there that I might have dressed the wounded, including my brother who received an arrow in the breast. My husband had now lost everything but his courage, honour, and perseverance.

The American consul, we heard, was delighted with our misfortunes. But in this delight he was alone!

3. A second voyage to Massacre Island; this time I accompany my husband. Contest with the natives. The appearance of Shaw, who was supposed to be dead. Account of his sufferings. Further hostilities with the natives. The castle is attacked; we decide to leave. The breadfruit tree.

CAPTAIN MORRELL NOW petitioned the governor for leave to take out a new crew of seventy additional men, sixty-six of whom were from Manila, that is, half-blood Indians who have all the jealousy of the Spaniard, tied to the cunning and ferocity of the savage. Everyone remonstrated against taking so many, but eventually my husband had his way and the men were shipped, and the schooner readied for sea, notwithstanding every effort against us by the consul. But the tooth of the serpent was broken as Messrs Cannell and Gellis advanced my husband all that was required to fit out the ship.

On 1 July 1830 the *Antarctic* was ready to sail again for Massacre Island. On boarding, I found a crew of eighty-five men, fifty-five of them as savage and potentially dangerous as those we were about to encounter. Even so, I entered my cabin with a light step – not fearing savage men half so much as a civilised brute.

The schooner itself now had ten great guns, small arms, boarding pikes, cutlasses, pistols, and a quantity of ammunition. The more helpless we are, the more we delight in viewing all the preparations for defence. But she now seemed a 'war-horse' in every sense of the word but that of animate life, though to hear the sailors talk she was that as well.

On 13 September we reached Massacre Island. I could only view the place as a Golgotha, but I could see that most of the old crew were panting for revenge. Mr Morrell endeavoured to impress upon them the folly of holding such passions if we could gain our purpose by mildness mixed with firmness.

As soon as we made our appearance in the harbour, we were attacked by about three hundred warriors. We opened a brisk fire, and they immediately retreated. Then we shelled where we felt the village to be. This was the first battle I ever saw where men in anger met men in earnest. Our Manila men were anxious to be landed instantly, feeling, no doubt, as much superior to these ignorant savages as the philosopher does the peasant. This my husband would not permit. He knew his superiority lay on board, a superiority that would be lost as soon as he landed. And so it proved.

Next morning a single canoe appeared with one man

in it, naked and highly painted, but managing his paddle with a different hand from the savages. Once alongside we recognised Leonard Shaw, one of our old crew supposed dead. The meeting had that joyousness about it impossible to be felt in ordinary life and we immediately made him recount his adventures. Shaw, wounded when the others were slain, fled to the woods, remaining hidden until hunger induced him to attempt to give himself up to the savages. But coming in sight of the spectacle of the bodies of his companions roasting for a cannibal feast, he again sought the woods with the intent to starve if necessary. For four days and nights he was forced to try somehow to obtain food, ultimately obtaining three young coconuts on which he subsisted for fifteen days, during which time he also suffered from continual rain showers. Having no chance to dry himself, on the fifteenth day he ventured to stretch in the sun, where he was seen and at once surrounded. He implored for mercy, but implored in vain as he was apparently struck on the back of the head with a war club. When he recovered, he made signs to one of their chiefs that he would be his slave if it would save him. The savage intimated to him to follow, which he did, the savage cruelly dressing his wound by pouring hot water into it, and filling it with sand. The next day, still in agony, Shaw was set to work in making knives and other implements from the iron hoops and other plunder from the *Antarctic*'s blacksmith's forge. This

Shaw found hard, for though a first-rate jack tar, he was no mechanic. However, necessity dictating he now become a blacksmith, he got along pretty well.

Then the savages made him march five or six miles to exhibit him to another chief. This was done in a state of nudity, without any sandals or moccasins to protect his feet from the flints and sharp shells, and under the intolerable sun. Blood marked his footsteps all the way, and at the end of the journey this new king compelled him to debase himself by the most abject ceremonies of slavery. He now became indifferent to life and ready to die. He could not, would not, walk back, as his feet were lacerated and swollen almost to a state of putrefaction. The savages saw this, and took him back by water. In the canoe he experienced yet new torments as the young ones, imitating their elders, began pulling out his beard and whiskers, eyebrows and eyelashes. In order to save himself part of the pain of this wretched process, he was permitted to perform this work with his own hands – to torture himself!

Back at the village he was almost starved to death, for they gave him only the offal of the fish they caught, and this but sparingly. He sustained himself mainly by catching rats, his principal food for a long time. And as the natives, for whatever reasons, did not suffer the rats to be killed he had to do this secretly in the night-time. Thus passed his days, his head not yet healed notwithstanding all his efforts to get the sand out of his wound. Then it was made known to him that he was to provide a feast to the king of the group! As all had now become a matter of indifference, he heard this with composure, watching as all the preparations were got up in his presence. Finally, all was in readiness, but the king did not come, and the ceremony was put off. Shaw said later that he felt at that time some regret that his woes were not to be ended as his constant state of agitation was already worse than death. Then the *Antarctic* made her appearance a second time, he now fearing her arrival would be the signal for his immediate destruction! As I have described, the whole population mounted their formidable attack, but were repulsed. But onshore their paroxysms of rage changed to fear when they found that our big guns were reaching their village and rapidly demolishing their dwellings. Plus the sound of these cannon alarmed every woman and child, they never having heard such a roar before, at which they sent off Shaw to sue for peace.

The story of Shaw's sufferings raised the indignation of every one on board, and all were violently desirous to attack the island, and extirpate this savage race. But Capt Morrell was not to be governed by any impulse of passion; he had other duties to perform and to try for a cargo for his owners and to make his voyage.

First he agreed a peace, and a wary trade began. Then he bought from the main chief, Hennean, one of the small uninhabited islands – purchased in exchange for axes, shaves, and other mechanical tools. This was named Wallace Island for one of those who had fallen in the massacre. Now my husband secured the ship by getting up boarding nettings many feet above the deck, and everything prepared for either defence or attack. Now the frame of a house, brought from Manila for drying the bêche-de-mer, was erected. My husband landed with a large force, under the guns of the ship, and finding two large trees, nearly six feet in diameter, cleared them of branches up to about forty feet from the ground, and extended a platform from one to the other, with an arrowproof bulwark around it. Upon this platform were stationed twenty men, with four brass swivels, and a good stock of provisions in case of a siege. The ascent was by ladder, which was drawn up at night. This platform had over it a watertight roof, and the men slept there with their arms. The next step was to clear the woods from around this castle, in order to prevent the natives coming within arrowshot. Next the drying-house was raised, being one hundred and fifty feet long, forty feet broad, and very high. So the castle protected the house with its workmen, and both house and castle were protected by the *Antarctic*, riding just offshore.

At dawn a few days later a large number of canoes began to gather near the ship. Shaw said he believed them from another island – he had never seen them before. My husband, having some suspicions, did not suffer the crew to go ashore that morning. At about eight o'clock, as usual, Hennean came off to offer us fruits, but my husband refused to send a boat to meet him. Hennean now directed his course to our small island. This was surprising, as not a single native had set a foot on our island since work began. We were not kept long in suspense, for now a hundred war canoes started from the back side of Massacre Island for Wallace Island. We prepared for battle.

Hennean now landed in front of the castle, gave the war-whoop, and about two hundred warriors, who had concealed themselves in the woods during the darkness of the night, rushed forward discharging their arrows at our castle till they stuck, like porcupine's quills, in every part of the roof. Our garrison waited silently until their assailants were within distance, then opened a tremendous fire from the swivels which were loaded with canister shot. The *Antarctic* simultaneously opened up with all her large guns, all with a deadly aim. The execution was great, and shortly the enemy made a precipitate retreat, taking with them their wounded, and as many of their dead as they could. The ground was strewed with implements of war belonging to the slain, or those who ran. They took to the water, leaving their canoes, while the Wallace Island garrison hoisted the American flag, greeted heartily by those on board as our victory had been achieved without no losses, and only two wounded. The music struck up *Yankee Doodle*, *Rule Britannia*, etc, the crew hardly restraining their joy.

The boats of the *Antarctic* were now manned, and most of the crew went on shore to observe the devastation which had been made. I saw all this without any fear, so easy is it for a woman to catch the spirit of those near her. If I had, a few months before, read of such a battle, I should have trembled. But seeing all the courage displayed, and noticing at the same time how coolly all was done, every particle of fear left me, and I stood quite as collected as any heroine of former days. Still, a part of me deplored the sacrifice of these poor, misguided, ignorant creatures, who were, however, of human form, and with souls to save. Must the ignorant always be taught civilisation through blood? But situated as we were, no other course could be taken. Our two wounded were dressed, and although at first we were apprehensive that the arrows might have been poisoned, they were not, and the men soon recovered.

On the morning of the 19th, to our great surprise, Hennean appeared at the edge of the reef calling for Shaw. He bore his usual air of friendship as though nothing had happened, and offered the usual fruit. A small boat was sent to meet him, but one heavily armed, while its coxswain had orders to kill Hennean if he suspected treachery. Shaw, who we feared was now an object of vengeance, was not sent in her. As our boat came alongside Hennean's canoe, the crew saw an arrow being fitted to a bow by one of the savages. The coxswain immediately shot him through the body, though he did not die immediately. At this instant a fleet of other canoes made their appearance, paddling furiously, and shortly after our small boat lost one of her oars in the fight. We had already manned two large boats armed with swivels and muskets, and a furious engagement ensued. The natives were driven ashore, taking Hennean, now wounded, who expired as he landed. After the death of Hennean the inhabitants fled from the island leaving all behind, and our men roamed over it at will. The skulls of several of our slaughtered men were found at Hennean's door, trophies of his bloody prowess. These were buried with the honours of war, the colours of the *Antarctic* were lowered half-mast, minute guns were fired, and dirges played by our band. Although millions have perished without such honours, it seems to be a passion of every age, nation, and religious creed under the sun to have funeral rites performed over the bodies of the dead. This love of posthumous honours is deeply ingrafted into our systems, as if implanted by nature. The last sad office that can be paid, and though last, not least.

We now commenced collecting and curing bêche-de-mer, and should have succeeded, if we had not been continually harassed by the natives, who now began to gradually appear again, culminating on 28 October 1830 when one of our men was attacked on Massacre Island, but escaped by shooting the brother of chief

Hennean. This man's name was Thomas Holmes, a cool, deliberate Englishman. Such an instance of self-possession, in such great danger as that in which he was placed, would have given immortality to a greater man. But constantly harassed and vexed, and finding it impossible to make the savages understand our motives and intentions, we came to the conclusion to leave the place forthwith. This was painful, after such struggles and sacrifices, but there seemed no other course to pursue.

Accordingly, on 3 November 1830 we set fire to our house and castle, and departed by the light of them, taking what bêche-de-mer we had collected and cured. If we had been left to pursue our course without molestation, there can be no doubt but that a fine voyage would have been made, for in no place is the article better or more abundant.

We soon arrived at Bouka Island, where, however, the manners and customs we found to be the same as at Massacre Island, except they have more formidable canoes, of better construction, which move more swiftly through the water. This island again abounded in bêche-de-mer and sandalwood, and if the people could be trusted, a good voyage, it was thought, could be made. But this was not to be.

Between these islands we encountered large quantities of sperm whale, as tame as kittens: probably no harpoon had ever been thrown at them since whaling began. All on board thought that these would be good whaling grounds, but those who visit these seas must be cautious how they expose themselves, as the savages are so powerful and treacherous.

Nature, kind mother and nurse to all her children, seems to have been very provident to these islanders of the southern and western Pacific, particularly in giving them the breadfruit tree. This grows wild on almost all islands within thirty degrees of the equator, but is in perfection from the tenth to the twentieth. It is a tall tree, about fifty feet in height, with spreading branches and large leaves, and makes an excellent shelter in the heat of the day. It bears fruit for three-quarters of the year in most places, and near the equator longer than that. The breadfruit is large and round, and about as big as an ostrich egg. Its pulp is only part eaten, and not raw. The fruit is generally cut into several pieces, wrapped up in an envelope of the leaf of the same tree, and put amongst the embers to roast for half an hour. Its appearance is that of the potato, its taste slightly of the tomato. This dish is mixed with the milk of the coconut and other vegetables. The same quantity of this food is more nutritious than either the plantain or bananas alone. A few trees supply a family, as the inner bark is fibrous, and can be used for cloth, fishing lines, etc, and the wood is good for making canoes as it is softer than our white pine when green, but grows hard by being thoroughly seasoned. And like the sycamore, it will last many years without decaying. This tree has been brought from the Pacific to the West Indies, and flourishes well there, but the Africans in slavery lose their taste for natural food in a great measure, and now prefer maize to breadfruit. The cultivation of it, therefore, is not much encouraged.

4. We visit New Ireland and New Britain. Warlike instruments of the natives. Island of Papua. Birds of paradise. Volcanic islands – new discoveries. Hostilities of the natives. Productions of these islands. Ambergris. Return to Manila.

We now shaped our course for New Ireland (3° S/152° E) and continued our way through St George's Channel, formed by the west side of New Ireland and the east side of New Britain (5° 44' S/150° 44' E). This channel has been described as one of the most beautiful on the globe, the hills on each side falling in from a lofty descent into the sea. The forests on these hills are of the most massy growth, and greatly diversified by various kinds of trees, intermingled with luxuriant flowers. The air is aromatic with nutmeg and other spices. These islands are said to be capable of raising almost everything in the known world, plus bêche-de-mer, hawksbill tortoiseshell, red coral, ambergris, pearl shell and sandalwood. We landed on New Ireland, and found a great variety of birds, some of beautiful plumage, and others of most melodious notes. Hogs and dogs were also plentiful. The fish are remarkably fine around the island. It seems to be a law of nature that where she deigns to shows kindnesses, she outpours abundance.

The natives visited us, bringing plenty of fruits and fowls, exchanged for a few pieces of iron hoops and some trinkets. Few people are better formed than these islanders. They are dark, stout built, and may, I think, become the most civilised in the eastern world, the happiest race of wild men I ever saw. It is amusing to think how soon we become enamoured with the thought of natural society, for in looking upon these forests and their inhabitants we soon compare them with the thousand evils of our own social life; here there is no vulgar wretchedness, no squalid diseases, no aristocratic contumely, while the laws of nature are only slightly regulated by convention or necessity.

From here we sailed to the north cape of New Britain where the inhabitants seemed of a much more savage nature than those of New Ireland. The shores are surrounded with coral reefs, about eight or ten miles from them. Arrowsmith's charts, my husband said, were pretty correct, but he regretted much that he could not spare time to produce a more correct one. It is wonderful to me that they are correct at all as so little time could be bestowed upon the subject. We sailed along the shore for some time, now and then having a difficulty with the natives who thought our vessel so small it could be taken with one or two canoes. But we had only to splash the waters about their canoes with a cannon shot or two to keep them at a distance. There seems to be something terrible to the savage ear in the sound of a big gun, and whose ear ever gets familiar to the roar of a full-mouthed battery? As a person I think myself quite brave, but must confess I always tremble a little to hear a great gun fired, and to feel the tremulous motion of the ship at its recoil.

We crossed the straits, and came close under the northern shore of an island that lies nearly in the centre of the strait, which my husband called Dampier's Island in honour of that great discoverer. The natives came off very cautiously, but by coaxing them with trinkets we got them alongside. They seemed to be more than usually inquisitive for savages, examining everything, and eager to know the uses of the chain cables and anchors, guns, everything on board. We purchased fishing gear, spears, war clubs, and pearl shells, plus some of their household implements, such as knives and other instruments made of pearl shell of no ordinary workmanship. They presented us with some elegant spears, with pearl-shell heads, and ornamented with fine carving and feathers of the birds of paradise. The wooden part of these spears is of excellent heavy dark wood resembling ebony and the carving really curious, bespeaking an advance in the arts hardly believable in savage life. It would be astonishing for those who think all barbarous nations are only on an equality in the arts with our North American Indians to witness such specimens of skill.

The villages of these islanders are laid out upon the sides of the hills, their dwellings shaded by lofty coconut and breadfruit trees. They seem to live happily among themselves, and to enjoy every hour of their existence. And as far as I am able to judge, they die naturally as I saw no victims of disease, nor any instances of decrepitude.

On 12 November 1830 we left Dampier's Island, and sailing at thirteen miles an hour, assisted by the current, soon reached the north of Long Island, which is less elevated than the one we had just left. We saw only a few wigwams along the shore, but could not conveniently land, and so proceeded to the coast of New Guinea.

We now reached De Kay's Bay (5° 39' S/146° 2' E). The villages around these shores are numerous and pleasant. The natives have the negro cast of features, though they are not in person like the negro, for they are well formed in their limbs. Although their appearance is as savage as could be, they are shrewd. But no one looking at them would confide in them for an instant. They are formidable in war, being expert in the use of the bow, and able to send their arrows with great directness and force. They are also extremely adroit in catching fish, a considerable part of their daily employment.

The heads of these natives are decorated with the plumage of the bird of paradise. We saw many flocks of these birds soaring high above the water, floating along like tufts of feathers, and sized from a pigeon to a sparrow. The noise they make is not at all melodious, but a sort of chattering without a distinct note. Yet nothing can look more beautiful when floating along with all the colours of the rainbow in the rays of the sun. They have such an abundance of feathers compared to their weight, that it is easy for them to keep on the wing, and therefore the romantic have made them live forever in flight. I believe that they flourish only near the equator, and cannot endure the slightest chill. They live among flowers and sandal-wood; delicate things are generally grouped together.

The race of men, of course, make an exception to this rule. But just as nature often revels in beauties where man is ignorant and savage, man is often greatest where nature is sterile and iron-bound. No bird of paradise ever spread its wings on the hills of North America, or the mountains of Switzerland or Scotland, where man has reached the highest moral and intellectual per-fection. And when civilised man takes possession of the bowers of Eden, he soon sacrifices every grace to the rigid laws of utility and productiveness. The most lovely streams in our own country, adorned with dashing falls and pure water, are soon stopped and tortured to turn a mill wheel, or dammed up to fill a canal. But utility must be paramount to taste, in a world whose object is gain.

On Saturday, 13 November in the afternoon we were close to a headland that seemed hanging over the sea. My husband told me to put the name of this cape (latitude 4° 59' S/longitude 145° 16' E) in my journal as Cape Livingston, in honour of Edward Livingston, Esq, Secretary of State. About six leagues from this cape north-northeast lies a small, active, volcanic island. At night, sublime flames burst from the crater, ascending much higher than those of Etna or Vesuvius, as those have been described to us, reaching at least a thousand feet. It was as if ten thousand lamps were suspended over our deck, and the volcanic stones cast up from the crater appeared like myriads of red-hot shot, but shot thrown up to incalculable distances. I gazed on this scene as one of wonderful sublimity, and thought how impotent language was to convey a full idea of it. The following day, on course for the island of Papua, we passed six other volcanic islands, all of which were at full blast.

The next day, 15 November, we passed another headland, which we called Cape Decatur, in honour of Capt Stephen Decatur, formerly of the United States navy. Then we fell in with numerous other islands, but I do not recollect that my husband gave them a name. These were low set in the water, surrounded by a coral reef, and had plenty of bêche-de-mer, pearls, tortoise, and oysters. From these islands the natives came off in great numbers and, by making their canoes fast to the *Antarctic* and paddling towards the shore, made an attempt to run us on the reef. But the wind being brisk, they could make no headway, and their lines soon parted. In their rage, they shot their arrows at the schooner. We, in return, fired a few guns over their heads. The report of the cannon astounded them, and many leaped into the sea. A boat was lowered while they were in confusion, and we picked up one of the natives for the purpose of educating him, by giving him an opportunity of seeing civilisation, and then returning him to his native country. These natives dress with coral necklaces, feathers in their hair, and numerous other ornaments, which give them quite a stylish appearance. Tortoiseshell and mother-of-pearl are profusely used, and they bear marks of opulence in all those things which we think of as important. Their dress is an apron about their loins, formed of several kinds of materials according to their rank. They are well formed and muscular, and their features manly. They are unlike any other tribe in these seas.

Finding a good passage through the reefs, we anchored, and while here my husband purchased several pieces of ambergris. I examined this wonderful substance very attentively. It is darkish yellow, closely resembling beeswax. It had insects and beaks of birds in it, and burned very clear, as does beeswax. When rubbed, it emits a perfume much admired. It is taken from the water, about one-third of it floating above the surface. Numerous accounts are given of its nature and origin. It has been said that it grows in the intestines of the spermaceti whale, but only in those that are poor and unhealthy. Whalers, however, have a general impression that it originates within the whales from the whales feeding on certain fish called squids. Orientals, for their part, considered it a sea mushroom. They think it grows on the bottom of the sea and, by time or accident, is rooted up and floats to the surface where it hardens by exposure to the sun. Others say that it grows on the rocks, and is washed off in storms. Some suppose it a form of honeycomb, which, by dropping into the sea, undergoes a chemical change. Others contend it is bituminous matter from the bottom of the sea. Others again think it the excrement of certain fish.

My husband, who has been much in these seas, is of opinion that the natives have a correct idea of the substance, viz, that it is made by an insect at the bottom of the sea, and accumulates for years; that seabirds devour it when within their reach, which accounts for their bills being found in it. The birds, being attracted by its glutinous qualities, strike their beaks too deep to extricate themselves, and their bodies decay, while the bony parts of their beaks remain. The sperm whale is a ravenous animal, and he may root it up and swallow it and this, perhaps, is one mode by which the God of nature intended that the leviathan of the ocean should be destroyed. That it is formed in the whale seems unnatural in many respects, the places, too, where it is found in the most abundance do not abound in sperm whales, and I have never read that it was found in any other kinds of whales.

But the poets of the East say that it is a gum from the tears of certain consecrated seabirds:

> Around thee shall glisten the loveliest amber
> That ever the sorrowing seabird hath wept,
> And many a shell in whose hollow-wreathed
> chamber
> The Peris of ocean by moonlight have slept.
>
> Thomas Moore

Whatever may be its origin, it has for many centuries been held in high estimation, particularly as a perfume and ornament, its use generally being confined to the rich and powerful. The price of it is astonishing. For, since the days of the rage for tulips in Holland and their high prices, there has not been a more fashionable whim among the rich than this partiality for amber, whether dug from the mines, or found floating on the water, or torn from the murdered whale. Perhaps this is the only way that commerce can be sustained, to supply the whims of the opulent as well as the honest wants of the community. I suppose the artificial wants of society support a great proportion of the people of every country.

We left these islands with a fine breeze, and on 26 November 1830 discovered islands from which we now took a further two natives, whom my husband named Sunday and Monday.

On the 27th we crossed a coral reef of several miles in circumference, with from three to ten fathoms of water, and from hence steered for the St Bernardino, which we entered on 10 December, and the next day touched at the port of Santa Sinto where we took provisions of which we were in great want, having been on 'short allowance' for many days. This I feared might create some disturbance but when the sailors and Manila men saw that we in the cabin were on 'short allowance' also, they were kept quiet as lambs. It is easy to govern others when we can govern ourselves.

During our whole cruise from Manila we had no sickness to speak of, only one man requiring medicine. This was effected by keeping all in a state of cleanliness, mainly by the use of vinegar; also by not allowing the crew alcohol, and by never allowing them to be long idle. So much is there in a spirit of good government that I have sometimes thought that tigers and lions might be tamed, if only they, too, were perfectly governed.

We reached Manila on Thursday, 14 December after an absence of about six months, and I went to sleep as quietly that night as if I had been in my native city. Next morning, however, as I apprehended, we found that our

evils were not at an end. For while our English and
Spanish friends were as kind as ever, still the consul
continued his persecutions. But by remaining close to
our vessel, and with the help of all our friends, all his
ploys and schemes could come to nothing

5. Stay at Manila. Visit convents and churches. Spanish ladies. History of the Philippine Islands. An earthquake. Singapore. Tour to the mountains. Effect of climate on English women. Singing birds. Perpetual summer here; winter at home. Horsburgh's *Directory*. Malays. Isle of France and Harriet Newell. The female missionary.

AFTER A MONTH we were ready, and sailed on 13 January 1831. It was hard parting with some of our good friends, as every heart responds to the old adage, 'a friend in need is a friend indeed'. Distance from home, too, enhances every kindness, just as it redoubles every insult. And while we had found friends among strangers, fifteen thousand miles from our native land, our troubles came from one of our own countrymen. Our government should be cautious what sort of men they send abroad, as people judge a whole nation from its representatives. I have said enough upon this subject, perhaps too much. Yet what I had endured pressed so grievously upon my heart that I could not be silent. I wished the world to know my sufferings, as their recital may serve a good purpose by putting others on their guard.

Before leaving Manila I visited several churches, and one of the convents. The churches are like those of old Spain, as they were built about three centuries ago. They have a solemn grandeur, but to a Protestant there is too much pomp and circumstance. Even so, the ceremonies are imposing. The paintings that ornament these churches are not so numerous as I expected, although some are said to be from the hands of great masters of Italy and Spain. I was at first inclined to think that paintings in churches were out of place, however solemn and scriptural, but I soon became pleased with examining them as works of art, and at times they made wholesome impressions on my mind, even in moments of my devotions. These large paintings, it seemed to me, also look better while the organ with its swelling peals is raising the soul to heaven by the divinity of music.

I must confess, too, that my impressions of a convent were not quite correct. Up to that time I had only known them as represented in novels, as the prison houses of beautiful girls who had been thrust there by proud or hard-hearted parents, and who would never again catch a glimpse of the world except through a grate of iron. But my visits to this cloister convinced me that a woman may be a nun even if old and ugly, as the greater proportion of the women I saw in this convent were solemn, staid and old. Now and then a young and handsome girl was seen, but bore no marks of misery about her, indeed, seemed composed, softened, and meditative, with no haggardness from weeping her soul away. All were fully occupied, some making clothes for the poor, and others were engaged in embroidering and painting, while everything that came from their hands had a nicety and delicacy about it as if wrought by fairy fingers. No, there was no idleness here as is generally supposed. Their devotions begin at the dawn of the day, and are often repeated during the whole of it in some form or other. But their lives are not more monotonous than most women in many parts of the world, where all the change in their lives, except such as age makes, is, as the Vicar of Wakefield says, from the blue bed to the brown.

Spanish women are well formed, though not possessing that extreme delicacy and refinement which our country considers as being necessary to exquisite beauty, nor can their complexions be compared with English or American ladies for whiteness and brilliancy. But there is a warmth of colouring in them that gives a sweet animation to their countenances whenever they are engaged in conversation, and no eye can be finer than that of the Spanish lady's. They are kind-hearted, and if vindictive, it is from 'love to hatred turned', or by some insult or neglect; nor are they wanting in heroic bravery as at Saragossa, while they love liberty and independence. They dress well, their clothes are rich and splendid, but they do not affect the French or English fashions and there is, as I have previously mentioned, a fine elastic step in the dance of the Spanish lady which is at once graceful, modest, and elegant.

Some of the ladies in Manila, from having Chinese domestics, have become in some measure acquainted with the Chinese language, and made some proficiency in writing it. They say that no people abound more in romantic tales than the Chinese, and I believe every nation has its region of fiction and storytellers, except our own, we having begun our existence with too much accurate knowledge to be under the necessity of having recourse to fiction.

Some of the Spanish at Manila are as near the days of Philip II in their manners and customs as some of our Canadian friends are to those of Louis XIV. There is the Moorish loftiness, often even among those in humble stations, while the Spaniard is also loyal to his king, shows no restlessness, lives frugally, and is content with what he has. He is quick and sensitive, and neither captious nor quarrelsome, but terrible in his resentments from wounded honour. The stories of assassinations are now and then true, but not a hundredth part as have been represented by the English and the

French. England, from the days of Queen Mary, has had no goodwill towards Spain, and since her time there has been no connection by marriage between the royal families of these kingdoms. England, on becoming Protestant, was obliged to seek alliances in Protestant Germany, and there had been no real friendship between England and Spain since the divorce of Catharine. And when England fought France in Spain, under Sir John Moore and others, it was rather from a union of purpose, rather than of feeling.

During my residence in Manila I witnessed one of those scourges of nations, an earthquake. At first there was no noise, but a frightful stillness in the air. The birds fell silent, and the whole animal world seemed to partake of the terror. The fishing families took to their boats, but I could not see a single line thrown out for fish. Initially, there was no motion of the water, but at length a gentle agitation took place, as if a heavy shower of rain was falling upon it. Shortly after, a rumbling was heard, resembling the movements of heavy-laden carriages at a distance on frozen ground. This increased, and the feet as well as the ear were affected with a motion something like that felt by a galvanic battery, or a slight shock from an electric jar. The leaves of the trees began a tremulous motion, the ground began to tremble, and some distant buildings were seen toppling down. The one in which I stood was only severely shaken and the wall did not crack nor give way. The great mass of the people preferred being in the streets, as they thought that there would be less danger there than of being crushed by the falling of walls. There was no screaming: everyone was too much terrified to scream. Some few were killed by the falling of houses, even while in the street. The people now began kneeling and saying their prayers wherever they could see a crucifix or an image of the Blessed Virgin, or flocking to the churches where Mass was being celebrated, men, women, and children sobbing and sighing, and prostrating themselves before the altar, thinking that the prayers of the clergyman could avert the Divine decree. From convents could be heard a low and solemn chant, rising and falling away again. There was not a word of courtesy to be heard, except what passed between the English and American people.

Now the rumbling noise ceased, and the shocks that followed made a noise more like the blowing up of a magazine of powder than of the movements of carriages on frozen ground. Fire, it is said, was seen to burst from the earth in several places. The agony was not entirely gone for nearly two days. In this time all business was suspended, and men, women, and children looked at each other as if it were the last time they would ever see each other's faces. Sometimes a tear stood in their eyes, but generally they were tearless as the marble statue. Great agitations in life, like all great griefs, are not relieved by tears.

The governor was constantly about on horseback, and saw that no confusion took place, while the priests did not take occasion to alarm the sinner, but soothed him by teaching him to trust in his merciful Creator.

The Chinese simply looked around with their little twinkling eyes, half-amazed, yet unwilling to retire from the scene of business while any remained to buy or sell. The Chinese are Predestinarians, and I was informed that they were quite unmoved, though remaining still and solemn while nature was in such throes and agonies.

The next day, after all was over, cheerfulness took the place of dismay, and a traveller just arriving could not have known that the people had ever felt a moment's anxiety. So are we constituted. For myself, I was alarmed, but not dismayed, and perhaps, as a stranger, I was in some small degree relieved, from not having any connections in the city, and from watching the movements of others in such perilous moments. Before leaving, I went to see some of the places from which it is said the flames issued at certain periods of the alarm.

And now we were finally on our long voyage home-wards. All hearts were light with thoughts of friends waiting in our native land. It was found, however, soon after our sailing, that our schooner was too deeply laden, and we altered course for Singapore (1° 17' N/103° 50' E) to lighten her and put her in proper order.

This city, which bears the same name as the island, is situated on the north side of Singapore Strait, and is one of the most delightful little places I ever saw. It is a fine location for trade, being in a central situation to all the numerous islands in the China and Java seas, and not far from the coast of China itself. It has sprung up almost at once by the magic of commerce. A dozen years ago, navigators tell us, there were but a few bamboo huts for the Indian fishermen, or perhaps a miserable Chinese huckster shop for those who might accidentally touch there. Now there are wide streets, fine sidewalks, and well-built stone houses, painted entirely white, all the work of the English. The materials for building are abundant and readily procured.

As well, it is beautifully situated, having all the advantage of a sea air, no stagnant water, and a fine back country. The forest trees are very large and tall, and on the south side is a fine plain, of great extent, and so highly cultivated it seems one great garden. The roads around and through this champaign country are excellent, and on each side of them are rows of trees and shrubs in perpetual bloom. The English merchant lays out and cultivates his grounds much to my taste, and a country seat here reminds an American that those who speak his language, and draw their information from the same sources, have been here.

The population of the island is extensive but the

precise number could not be ascertained. There is probably from fifty to sixty thousand of Malayo, Chinese, Siamese, and all that motley group of different nations that collect near a settlement of Europeans. The English population is about three thousand, and rapidly increasing by enterprising merchant-adventurers, and by the healthy situation for rearing children.

The Chinese here, as in other places in this quarter of the world, are the mechanics, and ingenious ones they are, and work very reasonably. The English merchants here give them better encouragement than they find in Manila, or any Spanish settlement.

The people under a tropical sun take most of their exercise at the dawn of the morning, when a ride or a walk is most delightful, for from the earliest dawn, dewdrops, shining and glorious with rosy light, are seen trembling on every tree, shrub, and flower. These dewdrops do something more than reflect the rays of light, they distil the sweet essences of all they fall upon, and the sense of smell is as much regaled as the sight. The odour is not like anything I ever remember, and comes not from one aromatic plant, but is the perfume of all 'Araby the Blest', and so ecstatic to almost overpower the senses. On one such ride we met a great number of English gentlemen and ladies on horseback, who parted with their native silence and gravity, so often remarked upon by other nations of Europe, to give us a most courteous salute. English women are truly beautiful. If they have lost some of their roseate complexion under these tropical suns, which in their native land gives some of them the appearance of almost rude health, they are compensated by fine forms and more interesting looks brought on by feeding more delicately in these climes, eating more vegetables and less solid food than in England. Their being at such a distance from their native land also seems to make them kinder, giving them a sort of fellow-feeling for strangers.

When the sun rides high in the heavens, these English return to their houses, remaining there quietly until the shades of evening and the dew begins to fall. This means the after part of the day is not so healthy as the morning. Yet how wondrous are laws of nature, that the tree and plant should drink up the poisonous part of the air in the night, and breathe it out a balmy res-torative in the morning!

On 23 January 1831 a party of us left the city to visit the highlands, about six or seven miles west of town. Leaving the public road, we found a pathway of ten or twelve feet wide cut through a thick forest, and made by great labour. It is as straight as the nature of the ground will admit and the forest trees are so large and spreading in their branches at the top that the road is nearly hid from the sun, and seems, a great portion of the way, as if dug through the hill, excepting that the forest admits, dense as it may be, a little more light than could be expected in a subterranean passage. The ride, although we were obliged to go at a snail's pace, was delightful. Birds of ten thousand hues were hopping from branch to branch, almost as tame as if in a cage so seldom are they disturbed. I had been impressed with the belief that the gayer the plumage, the more discordant the notes, but found here that feather has nothing to do with voice. We get such impressions in America from the notes of the peacock, and the woodpecker, but here the birds of emerald and sapphire hue have notes as sweet as their plumage is beautiful. I wanted to bring some home with me, but was told they would not bear the vicissitudes of the voyage. My husband and his officers offered to shoot all kinds for me. But as I was no ornithologist, and therefore could do nothing with classifying them, I could not suffer them to do this.

The horses, acquainted with the way, kept a sure footing, and in two hours we gained the summit. Its elevation from the sea I could not learn – not yet having been accurately ascertained – but it certainly must be more than a thousand feet. The view is bounded only by the horizon. The southern extremity of the Malay peninsula is in sight, and with a good glass as used at sea, as well as the peninsula we could stretch the eye over the highly cultivated plains, their flowering trees at this distance looking like shrubbery in full bloom. And as no scenery is perfect without a water prospect, here you may also behold the smooth waters of the

Straits, reflecting the scattered islands that seem to sleep on the surface, the whole prospect, as the painters say, in 'fine keeping'. Nor are the waters lifeless. The shipping of numerous nations is seen moving towards Singapore, while the little skiffs of the Chinese, built with no taste or shapeliness, are seen darting in every direction. Here is every kind of naval architecture, from the Malay prow up to the fine East Indiaman, this latter uniting size with beauty, majesty with storage.

On 23 January it occurred to me that while here we were enjoying perpetual summer, at home winter would now be set in, in good earnest, the earth covered with snow, and every brook, pond, and river bound in fetters of ice. And I asked myself in which of the two regions should I desire to live? For while here all may be constant fruition with no change in climate but the shifting of the wind, at home in winter we have long evenings of social intercourse, lectures and sermons for moral instruction, invigorating sleigh-rides, and the hopes of budding spring and summer again. But here, although life is not longer, most certainly health is better and more easily preserved. The inhabitants are not liable to colds which bring on that consumption which, physicians tell us, cause one-eighth of the deaths in our northern climate. I speak particularly of females. In all my intercourse with society in Singapore, I never saw a dyspeptic or a consumptive female.

When we returned that day I realised how fortunate we had been just to be able to make such an excursion. In America we might wander from the Catskill to the heights of New Hampshire and Vermont, as matters of ordinary occurrence. Yet seldom do navigators get to take such tours, or if they could spare the time in these regions it would, in general, be unsafe to try it.

To sum up: Singapore is stocked with pearl, tortoiseshell, ambergris, birds and animals of all sorts, the whole variety that belongs to the great eastern archipelago. It has fine water, and a most luxuriant soil, which the enterprising English are putting into cultivation. In fact, there is hardly a thing of a tropical growth that is not to be found there, plus a sufficiency of British capital and a considerable garrison. It lies in a very healthy situation and will, I am convinced, become the mart of traffic from all the Philippine Isles, which are more numerous than the Arabian tales, more than a thousand having been discovered and put down on charts, or mentioned in the voyages of navigators. And while in other eastern places the natives are fond of plunder, and extremely treacherous, here all is safe. For where the English and Americans are, there is no danger of evils from savage men. It is my belief that these two nations will govern the world, their policy and laws being adopted in regard to commerce in all countries, and with liberty extended to all nations, particularly in regard to the abolition of slavery.

On 24 January we were ready for sea, and a number of our friends came on board and took a sail with us for several miles, just far enough to make it pleasant, then taking their leave with great affection. We had received much hospitality, much more so than in crowded cities in old and populous countries. Here, every stranger is considered not only as a visitor, but also a sort of link between themselves and their native lands, and they naturally exert themselves for his happiness. As for females, the first person with whom she naturally forms an acquaintance in remote regions is the priest of her own religion, or with the physician, if she should happen to need one.

That evening we came to anchor in the Straits of Rio within a short distance of the shore, and the next morning sailed again through these straits, clearing them in the evening while still in daylight. This precaution is necessary from the numerous coral reefs scattered along the coast. A navigator cannot be too cautious: hundreds are lost from a want of carefulness.

On the 26th we found ourselves in the Java sea, and thence steered for the Straits of Sunda ($5°\ 55'/105°\ 53'$ E) and arrived at the eastern entrance thereof on the 28th. We sent a boat towards ashore, but seeing with our glasses that the natives were in motion, and suspiciously so, a signal was given from the *Antarctic* for her to return without landing. Formerly the natives were not hostile, but it is said that they now have the taste of blood. These seas are dangerous, and we stationed men at our bows with arms to prevent boarding.

The Malays are proverbially proud, treacherous, revengeful, and avaricious, but when met with spirit are not persevering in hostilities. Their climate makes them indolent, and, of course, they know little of the blessings of industry, and are too lazy to improve. Their dress is singular to us, but all civilised Asiatics resemble each other in dress. They are Mohammedans by religion, and wear turbans on their heads, differing but little from those of the Turks, but are more tenacious of religious observances than even the Turks. They deal in mysteries and study magic, pretending a great proficiency in that art, while their professed magicians, for aught I know, are held in as high veneration by the common classes of people as those of the olden time were at the courts of Babylon. Most of them carry charms and amulets about them, as preservatives against sorceries. Like all the eastern nations, they make ablutions a part of their religious ceremonies. It is said that the Koran prescribes all these ceremonies, and it does, but Mahomet found such customs prevalent among the people, and with great sagacity made them a part of his religious creed. The laws among the Malays are such as generally prevail with the eastern nations, only they come in a more barbarous form than those found in some others. It is also a great mistake with us to suppose that these Malays are ignorant of letters, as I have seen some fine pieces of chirography from them.

A great deal of information of these waters, and their peoples, may be found in Horsburgh's *Directory*, a work which my husband praised so highly that I studied it as a country justice does the *Farmer's Almanac*. This cool and intrepid navigator spent a good proportion of his life in these seas for the East India Company, and was a great matter-of-fact man, to which he added sound judgements and wonderful perseverance. The East India Company, whatever politicians may say about 'monopoly' and 'exclusive privileges', has done more to make safe the navigation of eastern waters than all the world besides.

Governments are not generally disposed to do much for the general interest, and our own has hardly made a chart for the navigator. I was mortified that in every country we visited, we sailed by charts of other nations, even leaving New York by an English chart. Nor had we any books on board written by our countrymen, giving particulars of these areas, although I understand one or two volumes have lately been issued upon this subject, but I have not seen them, and we had nothing of the kind when we sailed. It was to English books only we had recourse! Perhaps I am not wise enough to understand this. But I know that next to the English we are the greatest wanderers over the globe, and have as much at stake, from the north to the south pole, as any other nation *but* the English.

We experienced near Java Head variable winds and heavy thunder and lightning, until we took the southeast trades, which was about 12 February 1831. We were now once more in the Indian Ocean heading towards the Cape of Good Hope. The trade winds are a great curiosity. You find them blowing steadily for six months one way, and then they change and blow six months the other: but woe betide those who are caught in those seas at the time they are shifting, when the winds become variable, and storms of rain and thunder gather up and make navigation very difficult and dangerous.

We continued our passage to the south and west until we passed into sight of the Isle of France (Mauritius) (20° 2' S/5° 75' E). As we came near I most earnestly wished my husband to touch at it, for here, I understood, lay the remains of Mrs Harriet Newell, a missionary from New England – daughter of Mr Moses Atwood, a merchant of Haverhill on the banks of the Merrimack. Her family being highly respectable, Miss Atwood, as she then was, received a good education until, about the year 1806 or 1807, she became religious and active in piety. She began to correspond with others of a like mind, writing like one deeply imbued with divine grace, always a pattern of modesty and moderation, while still attentive to every domestic duty. Her name became familiar in all the churches, and when the United States Board of Missions for India selected several promising young gentlemen to be sent to the East, Mr Newell was one of them, and at this point became acquainted with Miss Atwood. Missionary labours were the constant subject of their conversation, and at length her mind became wholly engaged in this great cause. She and her friends prepared some articles it was thought might be wanted by those engaged in this perilous undertaking, which meant she often spoke to Mr Newell. He ventured to ask her hand, and to request her to share in his great work of saving souls. She had not contemplated this. Now she took advice of her friends and family, and sought direction from heaven, and although there were many doubts, and some opposition, she accepted him. It was enough to shake the firmest mind to leave home, part with mother, sisters and brothers, and a train of dear friends, but she put her trust in the Lord, and took her departure for the Indies.

'I never shall forget,' says one of her male friends, 'the hour of Mrs Newell's departure. The circle were engaged in prayer, and a clergyman with a harsh voice and strong lungs was leading in the devotions, he struck with no gentle hand, and the little group could not refrain from tears and sighs at the thought that they might never see her face again.'

When the clergyman ended, she, in a voice sweet as an angel's, began to speak to her distressed friends, representing that her beloved Saviour was everywhere a protector of those who obeyed his precepts, that he could soften the rage of intolerable suns, and break the iron heart of obdurate man, and that as life was short, and time for doing good limited, it was for each to commence his labours. She then commended all to God. Never had mortal words a kinder effect. The sobs ceased, the trembling voices of her friends assumed a firmer tone, and their farewells had no convulsions in them. As she turned to depart, her eye caught that of the narrator of this scene. They had once been intimate friends, but he, as a man of the world, had smiled at what he called 'the enthusiasm of the revival', and had seldom seen her after she left the gay circles of her youth. Now she stepped and stretched out her hand, which he grasped with emotion.

Then, with an affectionate smile, she said, 'My dear L, the time will come when you will think better of all this, while my prayers shall be for your conversion. Have no fears for me; I go on my Saviour's errand – may we meet in heaven.'

She gave them a benediction and went to India as Mrs Newell. Here she suffered much, finding more difficulties than anticipated. Her constitution was never strong, and she expired at the Isle of France, on 30 November 1812, in the nineteenth year of her age, living long enough to show the sincerity of her religious zeal, and her willingness to die in such a cause. If spared, she would have laboured assiduously in the great work she went out to perform, but as it was only had the chance to show the spirit within her. I understand an American shipmaster later found her grave on the Isle of France, without stone or name, and reared the best one he could for the time. In some future day, a traveller from the land of her fathers will build a proud mausoleum over her remains.

The world might censure the practice of sending out females with the missionaries, but I am convinced that men do little good without their wives and families. The ignorant natives feel the influence of example more than of precept, and when they see whole families living in peace and domestic affection, strive to imitate them. In the missionary's hut they see neatness, and all the little conveniences which exist there, and feel a desire for the same things, the native women first showing a love of dress, then cleanliness of person, every step of imitation being so much more gained in the march of civilisation.

6. Pass Madagascar for the Cape.
Luminosity of sea. Saldanha Bay.
Table Mountain. Comparison between
animals at the Cape and the race of
men. The albatross. Superstitions in
regard to the condor. Hottentots and
lions. The elephant. Ostriches,
description of, and their character.
Reflections on American ships and
trade.

WE NOW PASSED Madagascar, steering for the Cape of
Good Hope. In this sea, the phenomenon of the
luminous appearance of the surface of the water was
more remarkable than I have ever yet witnessed. At
night the sea appears one blaze of light. I watched this
extraordinary appearance many evenings as a subject
of curiosity and pleasure, and became anxious to know
what philosophy made of the matter. I looked at all the
books we had in hopes of finding the causes of it, but
after a while formed my own opinion upon the subject,
although I do not pretend to give it as one of certainty
where others have been in doubt.

Father Bourzes, a Jesuit, in 1704 marked this phenomenon in his voyage to India. Although going to a new world to help guide the heathen, he was also, according to the instructions of his order, obliged to notice everything remarkable in his tour. This pious father noted the singular appearance of the sea as I have described, but does not venture any reason for its causes. This class of men, the Jesuits, though subject to censure for so many years, have been the precursors of most of our knowledge of the world and of man. Among their faults was not that of apathy or ignorance. The finest descriptions of all nature came from these missionaries, the description of sea objects, soil, climate, cataracts, and prairies, came from them. They encompassed sea and land to make proselytes, and kept eyes and ears open in every step of their progress. Of their religion I can only say, it is not my religion.

This phenomenon was also discussed by the philosophers of Europe with considerable acumen, their first solution being electricity, which for a while was thought satisfactory. But on the voyages of Captain Cook in 1772, Mr Forster advanced a new theory which had so much plausibility that it was not questioned for many years. This was that this phosphorescence was caused by an animalcule analogous to the firefly, which had the power, at pleasure, of emitting light, and did so whenever the surface of the ocean was slightly agitated. This doctrine became general, for it was known there were many sea worms in the ocean that emit light. But the best opinion is now thought to be that of Mr Couton's that the appearance arises from putrefactions in the sea. The phosphoric appearance of a fish, a short time after he was caught, led Mr Couton to make many experiments. He put fish into a quantity of salt water, and marked the effects of their putrescence on the appearance of the water as they decayed. The decayed particles of fish, being lighter than the water, rise to the surface, and gentle agitation produces this light which makes so wonderful an illumination.

The wonders of land man has examined from the birth of creation, but of the treasures and population of the oceans, he has, as it were, just commenced his observations. The Earth with its nations of men, its beasts and birds, countless millions in all, has but a sparse population compared with the sea. If the death of these maritime creatures do 'incarnadine the sea', it is very natural once they have decayed and risen to the surface: another emblem that our frames, though sown in corruption, will rise in glory in another form. Yet is it not wonderful – miraculous – that such things exist in the waters under the Earth? Look at the whale, the leviathan of the deep, the whale, spouting and blowing, and initially a terror to man due to the tremendous majesty of his bulk, but which had no power compared with human sagacity, and whose very essence is now reduced to illumining the halls of men, and of chasing away the shades of night from the nursery of his babes. Is there any doubt that man had power given him over all that lives on land or in the seas? And which will always be there for the use of man, their master. For the whale fisheries in all parts of the world, although they furnish no small part of man's food yet there is no diminution of the stock. These great fish are no doubt diminished, but it is not in the power of man to destroy their race which, according to the best accounts, produce ten thousand, and even a million yearly, while millions of the cod are caught annually off the northern shores of America, without a diminution having ever been perceptible.

The analogy between things in the water and on the land has often been a subject of inquiry and discussion, and perhaps there is something in it. There are 'sea dogs', 'sea elephants', 'seahorses', but in many respects the resemblance is fanciful, while I do not believe the deep furnishes anything of the slightest resemblance to man, the lord of all, although, of course, we women have been complimented by our sisters: 'mermaids', a race I believe to be all females, even in fable. As to these latter, the wonders of the great deep, I believe, will never be fully discovered, but there is no necessity for indulging in creations of fancy when there is enough of fact to satisfy any one.

On 4 March 1831 we spoke to an East Indiaman from Canton on her voyage to London. Captain Gates, her commander, most kindly offered us any assistance we might stand in need of, but our provisions were abundant, and we could only acknowledge our obligations. There is a courtesy that grows out of circumstances which becomes a habit, and then passes to a principle. Those who have been in want know how to lend assistance to others, and every mariner, with all the foresight in the world, must at times be in want of the necessaries of life. The offers of Capt Gates were so kind, that I was almost sorry to find that owing to our superior sailing he was nearly out of sight in a few hours. How much happier would our lives pass on shore, if we were employed in offering kindnesses to one another, in watching to see what good we could do our neighbours. Selfishness seems to belong to great cities. It is not found where the inhabitants are few, or at least it is not so perceptible.

On Thursday, 10 March we came in sight of the Cape of Good Hope (33° 55' S/18° 24' E) but it was some miles distant, whence we steered for Saldanha Bay (33° 01' S/17° 57' E), seventy or so miles northwest of the Cape, and came to anchor there on 12 March.

All hands were as now as busy as the inhabitants of the city of New York are on the first of May: taking down sails, splicing ropes, mending, patching, darning, and cleaning. But it is not to be wondered our schooner should be so out of repair, now being away from home more than sixteen months.

On the 14th I accompanied my husband on shore, where we received a most cordial welcome from several acquaintances he had made before, and who were now anxious to show every kindness to his wife. The Bay of Saldanha is the place where the fleet anchored to protect seven thousand English troops under Sir David Baird, for the last conquest of the Cape: a fine place to anchor, as the Dutch garrison at the Cape was at too great a distance to give them any trouble while landing. And although the Dutch showed great courage, the action was soon decided, and the British have had possession of the Cape ever since. Cape Town is a fine stopping-place for ships on their way to India, and necessaries can be furnished at short notice. The place itself was discovered by the Portuguese in 1493, and was named by the discoverer, Bartholomew Diaz, the *Cabo dos Tonnendos* (the Stormy Cape) for he experienced much bad weather there. But his more sagacious monarch, John II of Portugal, renamed it the Cape of Good Hope, as he entertained the 'hope' of finding the way to India by doubling this cape, done soon after by Vasco da Gama. The Portuguese never formed any settlement at the Cape, they had but few people to spare for colonising any but the fairest portions of their discoveries. The Dutch, however, about 1650, took possession of it as a watering-place. They drove away the Hottentots, finding no difficulty in reducing this ignorant and miserable race to slavery. Hottentots are small in size, but much esteemed as slaves, for they are the most abject in the world. The Malays and other slaves, when goaded by ill treatment, show some flashes of resentment, but these abject Hottentot wretches have none.

The south and west of the Cape are washed by the ocean, and on the north a long range of mountains is seen, some of which reach the point of perpetual congelation. The population of the whole country is very sparse, not one inhabitant to a square mile. There are a great variety of soils, but drought is excessive at certain seasons, with no vegetation for many months in the year. When we were there we saw large tracts of country blooming with a great variety of flowers, which shortly after was as dry and sterile as a clay heap.

Table Mountain is one vast mass of rock rising in naked majesty three thousand five hundred and ninety-six feet! Its very look is frightful. Some persons, it is said, have reached its summit, but it seemed to me to be accessible to none but the great birds of heaven. Two of these, the condor and the eagle, are seen in the grey of the morning, poising around its summit as if in scorn of the powers of man. It is thought that they carry their prey to the top of this mountain to devour it in peace. After gazing a few minutes through a good glass, the mass seems too heavy for the earth, and you feel as though it must sink, and carry with it all around. The rock is of primitive formation, there since the birth of creation, and probably will stand there until 'Heaven's last onset shakes the world'. If this sublime mass had been near tasteful Greece, or poetic Italy, how much it would have assisted the writers of the works of the imagination! But Camoens[14] alone has made this region a subject for the muse.

It is worthy of remark that while the beasts and birds of this region are wonderful in size and strength, the race of men should be so inferior in their proportions. Until our times the eagle was considered by ornithologists as the bird of Jove, holding supreme sway over all the feathered race and described as soaring higher, and keeping longer on the wing, than all others of the air. In majesty, strength, and vision, he was said to have no compeer. Modern discoveries have robbed him of all this superiority both in these regions, as well as in the Andes. The condor is now enthroned in his place. Until this age, the condor was ranked among the creatures of fable, with the roc of Arabian Nights, or with the wonders of Gulliver. Researches have now shown the African condor is the head of the vulture tribe, his size being twice that of the American eagle. Some of them, indeed, have been measured with extended wings of twelve or fourteen feet. His claws and beak are in proportion to the spread of his wing. He has the scent of the common vulture, and the eye of the eagle, enlarged even in greater proportion compared with that of the eagle. As birds, condors are almost constantly on the wing, soaring at sightless distances above the earth and coming to ground only to secure food. In his food he is coarse and vulgar, and, notwithstanding all that has been said by the poets, so is the eagle. For the condor feeds on dead carcasses when they can be found, but otherwise attacks flocks and herds, and has been known to associate with others to attack full-grown bullocks. But from his very nature he is generally a solitary bird.

The condor has been caught at the Cape, and in South America, and brought to the United States, where he has been examined thoroughly. He is in every respect a wonder, and there are amazing stories among the Hottentots that these birds have been seen with an elephant in their claws.

Turning from the mountains to look over the ocean, a seabird of equal size and even larger wing, the albatross, may be seen daily. This creature is web-footed, resembling in some degree the domestic goose as to the shape of its head and body, but the bill is more hooked than that of the goose. The great length of wing gives the albatross superior swiftness to all other seabirds, and, large as he is, he skims with the fleetness of a swallow over the water, catching everything that comes in his way. It is amusing to watch his flight after the flying-fish, he turns so adroitly. He is a great feeder, and sometimes acts the glutton to such an extent as to be easily taken while resting on the smooth surface of the sea. The albatross appears to have no regular home, but courses over half a world, and is found not only at the Cape of Good Hope, but also in Austral seas. He clears a storm by rising above it, keeping himself there until the whirlwinds have passed away. The albatross is tame, but not courageous, for he is often beaten to death by smaller birds, and makes but a feeble resistance. The extent of their wings when spread is generally ten or twelve feet, but they can grow to a much larger size. They are never taken for food, even by the Indians, being too coarse and oily. These birds are seldom killed by American or European sailors, as there is a mariners' superstition that it betides ill-luck to kill them, and it requires a brave man to oppose superstitions entertained by mariners, especially as all the misfortunes of a voyage are always charged upon any violence done to a settled prejudice.

Coleridge, the poet, made much use of this superstition in the *Rime of the Ancient Mariner.*

> At length did cross an albatross,
> Through the fog it came,
> As if it had been a Christian soul,
> We hailed it in God's name.
>
> A good south wind sprang up behind,
> The albatross did follow,
> And every day, for food or play,
> Came to the mariner's hallo!

'God save thee, ancient mariner,
From the fiends that plague thee thus!
Why look'st thou so?' With my crossbow
I shot the albatross!

And I had done one hellish thing,
And it would work 'em woe,
For all averred I had killed the bird
That made the breeze to blow,
'Ah, wretch!' said they, 'the bird to slay
That made the breeze to blow!'

At the Cape, the earth, as well as the air, teems with
wonders. The lion found here is the largest and fiercest
in the world, and although driven from many places still
holds his ground in South Africa. And although his roar
is often heard, he rarely make his appearance near the
habitations of men, and never attacks a man unless
famished, when his hunger is superior to his courage.
Many an officer in these regions has, with the help of
natives and dogs, gained laurels for bravery in lion
hunting who did not risk much in the contest.

The ponderous elephant is also afraid of man. Whole
droves of elephants will pass within a few rods of a
hunter without giving him the least fear. From the
enormous tusks which are brought to this market from
the country, the size of the giant of the forest may in
some measure be calculated. Some of these tusks weigh
over a hundred pounds.

Another wonder is the ostrich. These are plentiful, and many are offered for sale at the Cape by the natives. A full-grown ostrich is from eight to eleven feet in height, and the most awkward looking bird ever seen. Some portion of its feathers are delicate and beautiful, and were used as an ornament for female headdress probably before the records of man began, and as they were when Vasco da Gama discovered the Cape. And would now be if the native were not slaves, or if those who were not bondmen, and bondwomen, had not found that these plumes could be exchanged for something which they preferred to ostrich feathers.

The ostrich is often hunted, but they are still to be found in great numbers. Their eggs are served up at every great feast given among the officers of the garrison as a delicacy. Modern writers have stated that the ostrich incubates her eggs, and has as great a regard for them as any other bird, but this assertion appears to me unfounded. The ostrich cannot sit upon her eggs, there is no joint in her legs that will allow her to bring her body upon her nest. Job is worth a hundred philosophers upon the subject: 'Gavest thou the goodly wings unto the peacock, or wings and feathers unto the ostrich? which leaveth her eggs in the earth, and warmeth them in the dust: and forgetteth that the foot may crush them, or that the wild beast may break them. She is hardened against her young ones, as though they were not hers.'

An officer who had spent the better part of his life in Asia once gave this solution of the subject. The ostrich starts from the forest to the desert to deposit her eggs. She lays two, which she deeply covers with the sand, then seven or eight more, which are but partially covered. The first two produce young ones, who, as soon as they have broken the shell, begin to feed upon the roasted eggs which have been deposited there for food, until they become strong enough to set out for the wilderness. They are so fleet of foot and tireless, that hunters, in catching her, must use one fresh horse after another until the ostrich is exhausted. It is a most extraordinary fact, that the stomach of this bird, made, as it is said, to consume fruits alone, should have such powers of digestion as to consume lead, iron, or almost any other metal. Those brought to the United States are generally destroyed by trying this experiment too often. This bird is good-natured and, the ancients thought, marked with folly. But modern times have learned to discriminate awkwardness from folly, and adroitness from wisdom. It is said that when the ostrich hides his head among the weeds, he thinks he is not seen, yet does not even the wise man do pretty much the same?

The Hottentots have no fears of any wild animal. They contend that all animals are afraid of man, and this is probably the case. The almost naked African traverses the deserts or the forests as fearlessly as if he had dominion given him over the fowls of the air and the beasts of the field as it was given to Adam in the days of primeval innocence.

The garrison here is large, and is composed generally of well educated men, a much better society than under the Dutch government. The staid and solemn character of the Dutch may make a place a good permanent residence, but they do not give any of that spirit which makes a place delightful on a short visit. They catch not the graces of the passing hour. I speak of those who have lately come from their native land. The descendants of the Dutch in my own native state are not only among the most solid portion of the community, but also make up a highly respectable part of fashionable society.

The Cape of Good Hope promises, under its present auspices, to be an opening for civilisation to enter Africa, as not half of the wonders and the treasures of this country are as yet known. Nor, regarding trade, has as much been made of southern Africa and India as might have been if they were free, and no monopolies known. It is not only injurious but degrading to say you must not buy here, or sell there, but under a thousand restrictions. The world should be open for all, on equal terms, with no particular set of men able to enjoy extraordinary privileges, nor any nation to be particularly favoured. There are but few places, thank heaven, where an American vessel cannot go, and few indeed they have not visited.

At home, we females think but little of national glory or, rather, not much of the means of supporting it. But once abroad we become interested in everything connected with commerce, or naval power. A woman in these distant seas would be as proud to point to a fine frigate, or a seventy-four, from the United States, as she would in dwelling on the fame of Washington, or any other distinguished man of our country. The feeling of nationality comes over us when abroad, but we leave it for others to support when we are at home. At home, a female feels herself lost in the great mass of her countrywomen, but when abroad she represents them all, and must be dull indeed if she does not understand this situation. I was the first American woman who had visited some of the places I have described, and being a subject of curiosity, no one could be indifferent to such a situation.

7. Departure from the Cape. Sight of St Helena. Something of its history. Its military strength. Tomb of Napoleon – reflections at his grave. Recrossing the equator. Calms at sea. Dreadful privations possible through lack of water.

AFTER BEING WELL supplied with refreshments, and putting everything in order, we sailed on 22 March for St Helena (5° 40' S/15° 55' W). On the 28th we took the southeast trade winds, always delightful, and on 6 April came in sight of this 'prison-house in the sea'. The island first appeared as a cloud in the heavens, and I gazed upon it steadily until my imagination gave it almost every shape that a cloud could assume, from a whale to anything monstrous, but never like a weasel, excepting, as Polonius would say, 'it is black like a weasel'.

But on drawing nearer it assumed a more solid looking form, and eventually we anchored in front of Jamestown Valley. I had ransacked all our books on board to get an account of this wonderful island, that I might compare their descriptions with my own observations. It is unquestionably of volcanic origin, and was one of the early productions of omnipotence in those seas, ages before man had ever navigated them. It was discovered by the Portuguese, pioneers of navigation, on St Helen's Day, 21 May 1501, and is about twelve hundred miles from the African continent, entirely detached from any other island, reefs, or anything but the mighty Atlantic Ocean. Twelve years after its discovery it became the residence of an exiled Portuguese nobleman, who made some improvements in order to make it habitable. On being restored to favour he returned to his country. A few years later the English examined it, but did not think it worth possessing until after the visit of Cavendish in 1588, who made some additional improvements. St Helen, from whom it is named, was the pious mother of Constantine the Great, and as Great Britain had not entirely lost her partiality for saints, the name was not changed. The Dutch made claim to it, but chose instead to found their colony at the Cape of Good Hope. In 1657 Oliver Cromwell gave the East India Company a charter to govern the island, which was later made a 'royal' charter by Charles II. In 1673 the Dutch East India Company took control but were driven out by English reinforcements sent to the island.

The island itself seems less extensive than it is, probably because of its great height, rising, as it does, from the sea in an almost perpendicular wall up to twelve hundred feet. A great number of waterfowls hover around its mountains, or on the coast where the rock walls fall into the sea.

It is more than ten miles long and six broad, making not far from twenty-eight miles in circumference. There are only four openings in the great walls of this castle island, and from these full-mouthed batteries are pointed, with artillerists standing by the guns with match in hand. What are great guns wanted for here? And yet in every spot where a cannon can be placed, one of large size is to be found. It would seem that if only a common stone were thrown from these towering battlements, it would sink a ship. And what could the navies of the world effect against this castle island?

On landing, we ascended by one of these openings of nature, called James's Valley. This is a fruitful spot where the fig, orange, date, and pomegranate trees grow in great beauty, and the usual kitchen vegetables flourish abundantly. The water is good, and can be made to irrigate every part of the plains. The gum tree is still common on the island, although many of them have been destroyed, and the lofty cabbage trees grow in great luxuriance. On the high grounds the willows seem to hang as though they were clinging to the lowland brooks.

The place is equally wonderful in its history as in its situation, and was once stocked by a colony of those who were burnt out in London in 1666, and who in their desperation sought asylum on St Helena. James's Valley takes its name from James II, after whom also the fort was named. The town in this valley, Jamestown, has quite a picturesque appearance. The churches, for there are two (but only one parish), and the snug-built houses perched so high in the air, and yet low compared with heights still higher, produce a fine effect. An elevated chain of mountains divides the island into two unequal parts, but there are numerous ridges and valleys of greater or less extent. Diana's Peak is the highest part of the island, and commands a most superb prospect. From here you can see everything on, or about, St Helena. The ships look like small craft floating at the base of a tremendous castle, and the albatrosses, gulls, and other seabirds, skimming halfway from the sea to the height of this mountain, make the whole a fine panorama, one that nature seldom affords. There is also a fine aqueduct leading down for more than a mile to the water, very convenient for the shipping, who often stop here to replenish their casks, as well as their fruit baskets. Great pains have been taken to make good roads, and the success has been astonishing. Industry and perseverance, with wealth, can almost work miracles.

A fine assortment of goods may be found in the shops, and there is much more custom here than one would imagine. I bought several small articles, and priced a number more.

The cattle here, as well as the sheep, are good. The air they breathe is so pure, and their food is so sweet, that the beef and mutton are better than in any other place in the same latitude in the world. But when large India fleets arrive at the island, the price of beef is high. St Helena has now become a regular calling-place for the ships which traverse the Indian Ocean, and it is said that not less than one hundred and fifty of them arrive there in a year.

The poultry is also very good: chickens and ducks very sweet and tender, and in abundance, the people of the island taking great pains to raise them for the garrison, and to supply passing ships. The birds are not so various or numerous as at other islands I have visited, but the canary is here. A sweet songster, delicate, yet hardy bird, that will live long if taken proper care of. In this island they are too common to be an object of attention among the tasteful, but it must be confessed after all our discussions upon slavery, that a good canary bird in a cage, educated by man, is a more beautiful singer than those who live in the retreats of nature. They may be taught from various instruments of music, and made to surpass nature by the assistance of art.

The place seemed very healthy, yet upon inquiring I could not find one person verging towards a hundred years of age. This is not uncommon in our own country, where we suffer extremes of heat and cold. But here the air is mild, not rising much above summer warmth, and with only a change of a few degrees from one season to another.

Longwood is situated towards the northeast side of the island, on a plain raised seventeen hundred and sixty-two feet above the surface of the ocean. Here abounds vegetation of various kinds, but when I first visited it, I took no more notice of the beauties of nature than I should of the richness of the furniture in a room where a dear friend was laid out for burial. For it was here that the Emperor Napoleon was for several years confined, and where his ashes are now entombed. There was something in this that seemed at first to exaggerate the grandeur of the scene, and give it a deep and solemn cast that blended together the moral, historical, and the wonderful. It was only after a while that I could enjoy both the beauties of the scene, as well as contemplate the history of him whose name has conferred im-mortality on this spot.

Seeking his tomb, I found an iron railing around a flat, dingy-coloured stone, raised but a few inches only above the surface of the ground. A wooden railing encloses the iron one, and within, three large willows overshadow the grave. We marched up to the spot, took a twig of willow, and ordered one of our attendants to bring us some water from the spring whence the mighty emperor drank daily. It was sweet water, and as I drank, I thought of what old Cotton Mather said in his works, that the great virtues of cold water will not be made known to us for a thousand years to come.

As I bent over his grave, all the marvellous events of Napoleon's life came into my mind. Born on an island, he died on an island; both birthplace and burial ground are famous in history, with he more famous than all. I saw him a spirited cadet, a proud subaltern, a general in Italy, a commander in the Levant looking up to the Pyramids to catch their glory. I followed him through fields of blood, until I saw him disperse the corrupt legislature of France, and commence what philosophers called the parallelism of the fire and sword, his proud spirit growing still prouder until all the world cowered and bowed before his presence, as in his saloon maps of empires were laid before him and he drew levies of kingdoms as if in sport. I saw him placing the diadem of France upon his brow, and then the iron crown of Italy as empires fell before him, and ambition took possession of his soul. I saw him repudiate Josephine, and become allied to the house of Austria. I saw the genius that guarded him to a hundred victories become capricious in Spain, and desert him at Moscow. At Waterloo, the destinies were against him, and his fate was to die in this remote prison, to sleep under the humble stone before me.

That a man whose nod gave law to nations should now rest in this quiet little place seemed to me as a dream. A good place, thought I, to reflect upon the value of life, and the instability of fortune, reflections made upon the stone itself, for I was enabled to get within the railings to a position which few have enjoyed.

I made many inquiries respecting his treatment, but people were not inclined to say much. I found, however, that Sir Hudson Lowe, his gaoler, was not a favourite with them. My inferences, added to what I had heard, satisfied me that some insults, to say the least, were offered to the Emperor, but not from the people, for they now speak kindly of 'General Bonaparte', who was liberal to all allowed to approach him. He came to this place a fallen man, and so there was but little of that reverence the world pays to greatness ever felt for him at St Helena, nor were the people well pleased to think that their island would hereafter be considered as a prison.

The house in which he lived is now converted to a granary, and I believe that there are horses stabled there! But whether this is accident, or pitiful design, I do not know. It could not have been from any order of government, for they built him a new and more convenient house, to which he would not remove. He felt the death-fang in his heart, that all would soon be over with him. If he had not had an anatomical disease of the breast, disappointed ambition must have bowed him to the grave sooner or later

The conversations of Napoleon which have flooded the reading world were, no doubt, in part authentic, but it is questionable whether he was indulging in his own reveries, or sporting with his listeners' credulity. All the communications he could make to his friends were verbal ones, of course, as the eye of the police was too vigilant to permit any other. It is said that he seldom mentioned his wife, whether he thought that she was wanting in affection in not offering to accompany him in his exile, or whether he ever had any affection for her, is not known. Those who analyse say that no two mighty passions can exist at the same time in any mind. Ambition will destroy avarice and love, although the latter may master both the others.

The good people of St Helena are quite astonished at American enthusiasm for Napoleon. They say: 'He was no friend to republics, nor ever discovered any partiality to the people of the United States! And loved the trappings of royalty, and spurned everything that did not partake of aristocracy.'

Our answer to this is we neither feared nor hated him, and we could view him as a wonder in the history of man – as something above the ordinary dimensions of nature: a chastiser of nations, some of whom deserved their chastisement; a lover and patron of the arts and sciences, and a protector of men of genius; a destroyer of the last remnants of the feudal system. And finally, many of us viewed him as an instrument in the hands of God to promote unforeseen good to men. In short, that everything great is intended by its Maker for some great end. But I was never entirely satisfied with my own excuse for my enthusiasm for Napoleon: perhaps his noble physiognomy played some part in my admiration. For in every picture, bust, or statue, whether young and spare, or older and corpulent, his countenance is one of the noblest ever formed.

We left him, and St Helena, on Saturday, 9 April 1831, steering north with a delightful breeze. I kept my eyes directed towards the island, still thinking of the mighty dead and it came to my mind that the place was a fit one for the tomb of Napoleon, for there was something analogous between St Helena and himself. The mighty mass of stone was an instantaneous creation by volcanic power, and Napoleon arose by the eruption of the French Revolution, and they had hardly done wondering at his fortune when his reverses overtook him. But his fame will last as long as the rock on which he lies. History has already placed him alongside of Caesar and Alexander. And if the poet should sarcastically add: 'He left a name at which the world grew pale, / To point a moral, or adorn a tale' (Johnson, *Charles XII of Sweden*), still Napoleon will furnish the schoolboy with matter for a thousand years to come, while the historian will kindle with some of the enthusiasm we now feel at the mention of his name.

Our minds, after leaving a magnificent scene, or contemplating the achievements of a hero, experience a void that gives a restlessness to our spirits. The best cure for these feelings that I could ever find, when at sea, was to survey the immensity of waters, or turn to some sublime parts of the Scriptures. The contemplation of justice, mercy, and truth soothes our agitations, as there is a beauty in holiness which absorbs all minor interests. As eternity is beyond time, so are these subjects beyond those that lie in our pathway through life. There is something ever new to be found in the Scriptures, some new thought that will spring from every text. I do not believe there ever was a mutiny on board of a ship where the Bible was read diligently by the crew. Works of fancy can grow tedious from absorbing too much of our attention at once, but the Scriptures compel us to direct our reasonings and views to ourselves. If there ever was a book which could be called an awakener of our thoughts, it is that which furnishes so many thoughts for us: the Bible.

I have read it where Christianity was professed, followed, and held the highest claims to attention; I have read it where superstition abounds, and where infidelity, pagan infidelity, darkened the whole land: it was the same heaven-illumined page everywhere, but if ever peculiar glory rested on it, it was when we were near those who had never received its glad tidings, and who never knew the true God.

On 19 April we crossed the equator, but we were now all such old, experienced sailors that Neptune did not think it worthwhile to pay us a visit. And if he had come on board, he would have found our stock of liquor nearly the same as when he saw us before, except a little which had been used as medicine. And if he had brought his logbook, which sailors say he keeps of all bad deeds done during his absence, I question whether he would have found a single oath recorded, or one vile or blasphemous expression from any member of the *Antarctic*.

We had now many calms and baffling winds. There is nothing so distressing as a calm at sea. Lying like a sleeping tortoise upon the water, the vessel that at other times seems to have its own life, now loses all animation. Or, if there be a slight motion, it is a sea-sickening sort of one. The sailors become torpid. As it would be cruel to set them to hard work under a tropical sun, they, too, lie about as creatures without soul or spirit. In such a situation the nights are restless, the days endless. All that memory can furnish, books can supply, or conversation can offer, is nothing. Everybody feels dissatisfied, and you see yourself reflected in every face. You cannot laugh an hour away, and if you smile, it is like Cassius who scorned a spirit that 'could be made to smile at anything'. If, gentle reader, you have an enemy, you can never wish him anything worse than a calm at sea. The sun seems to rise in wrath, and set in fiery indignation, and the only thing unchanged was my husband's patience, which was proof against all.

And what of the sufferings of those who are in want

of good and wholesome water at such times? We, thank heavens, had a good supply of both water and provisions, and still these calms were dreadful. The tales of distress we have read about such times, however horrid, are, I believe, only half told.

At length on 13 May we took the northeast trades, and were wafted along so sweetly for eighteen days until we arrived at Terceira, a passage that hardly seemed as long as one of those days in the calm.

8. The Azores. Liberia. Effects of exploring expeditions. Missionary societies. Effects of intoxicating liquors. Indians unacquainted with intemperance until taught by Europeans. Intellectual character of the Indians. Their ferocity ascribed to ignorance and ill-treatment. Arrive Cadiz. Not allowed to land as two of our men had died of cholera.

TERCEIRA IS ONE of the Azores Islands, a group lying in the Atlantic Ocean, about 36–40° N latitude, and from 25–35° W longitude. The Portuguese took possession of these islands in about 1446. The group is nine in number, some writers make more, by taking into the account some large rocks, but there are only nine islands of consequence, the principal one being Terceira, twenty-five miles in length, fifteen in breadth, and about fifty-four in circumference. The island is volcanic, the soil is productive, and oranges and grapes grow in great profusion. The climate is healthy, and though earthquakes terrify the inhabitants, it is seldom they cause any essential injury. It is the opinion of some philosophers that these islands are supported by volcanic arches, whose vast ovens are burning with perpetual fires, no very comfortable thought. But the inhabitants of the Azores think them the garden of the world, and it is assuredly true that a finer climate can hardly be found. Now having seen islands of the sea through more than three hundred degrees of longitude, they appear to me to have been brought forth by volcanoes in both oceans of the east, and of the west.

These islands were once supposed to belong to Africa, but of late years they have been classed as European, for now the inhabitants are Portuguese, whose government, though arbitrary, is mild. I could find no instances of oppression. The Portuguese are a quiet and inoffensive people, but hardly acquainted with the growth of America, which they still think in its infancy, as they measure all growths by length of years.

They have heard of Liberia, our settlement on the coast of Africa, and speak of it as a feeble attempt by us to get rid of our surplus black population. But we have other hopes, and I feel persuaded that this is one of the most important colonies ever planted since the settlement of North America. The climate of Liberia is as healthy as any we have known, notwithstanding the location, and with possibilities for unbounded territory, for a tenth part of Africa is not under cultivation. As well, the settlement is increasing as fast as did any of the

American colonies – with greater commerce in proportion to the number of inhabitants. And I can see nothing to prevent this colony from being a nucleus of nations, flourishing in arts, sciences, commerce, civil freedoms, and all that constitutes a state. What can be more rational than noble efforts to advance the interests of man, particularly degraded man? America and its people doing something to wipe off a dark spot from their escutcheon. The settlement itself came into being through the talents and perseverance of the agents and governors of the Colonization Society – especially the Rev Lot Carey, an extraordinary man, who died not long since at Monrovia. He was a slave in Virginia, who, by his own industry learned to read and to write, and was entrusted with the management of a large tobacco warehouse. By his perquisites and abilities he accumulated a sufficient sum to purchase not only his own freedom, but that of his wife and children. He was discreet, sober, and a preacher of the gospel while yet a slave; his views of the Bible were thought to be excellent. When the Colonization Society was formed, and Liberia purchased, he departed with the earliest settlers, and took his share in every labour. He acted not only as a spiritual guide, but as a civil magistrate, deputy agent, and for a while as chief magistrate of Liberia. In every situation he evinced the high powers of a gifted mind and righteous man. If such specimens of intellect and virtue can be found among slaves, what may we not expect from these people in a state of civil and religious freedom, enlightened by schools in every branch of knowledge?

But these expectations can only be realised by finding and instructing the heathen, which in turn means exploring expeditions, missionary societies, and universal temperance. Exploring expeditions should be got up by individual enterprise, assisted by government. For, of course, according to the present law of nations, discovery gives the right of possession, so far as it relates to any other power than the aborigines. And certainly, trade with lands discovered would be of advantage to our commercial people. It were well, too, that we should do something for the world whose commerce we enjoy. Our nation now has a name to support, but what have we done to raise its glory? Our whalers have accomplished something worthy of remembrance, but this is all. To Nantucket, New Bedford, Stonington, and a few other places, is most of the credit due for all the discoveries we have made in the Pacific Ocean. These enterprising men have traversed every sea in search of whales, and have generally communicated to the world what they have found to be new or profitable. They have opened their very accurate and satisfactory journals, and if no advantage has been taken of their discoveries, it is not their fault.

The next step is furnishing the means of instruction to savage men. This can only be done by sending out enlightened missionaries. Wherever an intelligent missionary establishment is to be found, there good results have been witnessed, notwithstanding the abuse of some, and the fear of others. Missionaries should also be sent to every isle of the sea as well as to the continent. Letters should be first taught, with domestic arts, and then the high principles of morality and religion.

Day schools and Sunday schools for men, women, and children, should be established. I firmly believe that the work of refinement and morals could go on rapidly in any of those islands which we have previously visited in the *Antarctic*, many, alas, still in darkness. The natural capacity of savages is not inferior to any people in the world. It is, I think, a law of nature, that wherever there is a fine physical organisation among mankind, there, also, will mental capacity be found. This may be a mortifying doctrine to old clans, tribes, or nations, but it is nevertheless true. I believe there is as much genius in some of the Pacific islanders, as can be found in France, England, or America. I do not believe that He who made man has given any particular gifts to one race. If there be any superiority, it is in His giving to some of the islanders a larger corporeal frame than to any other race that history has yet enumerated. The progress of the improvement of these people depends on us, and it is we who shall be answerable for any intelligence and virtue they come to possess. Much may be done at a little expense, for there are persons of good education who are willing to settle at these places if they could have the protection of government and the assistance of the charitable. The English language will in a few years be the language of all islands where English or American missionaries are established, for as soon as the natives become enlightened, they will find that their own scanty language to be insufficient to express their ideas, and will be anxious to gain something more, day to day, until they become proficient. They are, as I have said, imitative, and would soon learn to write well, like the Pomare, reaching a proficiency of which a professor of penmanship might be proud. However, the sole object must be to do good. Missionaries must have nothing to do with trade – that must be left to others. For if these people once get the idea that the missionaries are labouring to gain wealth, that moment their influence is at an end, and their only protection will be to resort to arms. It is not from a bloodthirsty disposition that the natives make attacks on vessels that visit them, but from a desire to obtain in the easiest way what others have.

On the question of ardent spirits! Civilised nations have heretofore carried intoxicating liquors to all those they visited, and thereby brought with them the vices found in the corrupt associations of the civilised world, vices that these poor ignorant wretches acquire before they had been taught a single virtue; civilisation thereby being a curse instead of a blessing. Ardent spirits have, in general, been an important article of traffic in these regions, the natives being cheated while intoxicated. It is the sweet recollection of our voyage that we have never offered to the lips of primitive man one drop of spirits. We have met them, and drunk the waters of their springs, and never told them there was anything they might like better. But apart from ourselves, it has been, so I am informed, the universal practice to carry liquor to the people of the Pacific islands, with dreaded and baneful effects. This offence should be made penal, as well as moral. Visitors to these benighted regions should never know such a thing as a drunken man ever existed. It is said by some that they already have inebriating liquor, but this is true only to a certain extent, and that a small one. Travellers may say what they please of natives in regard to intemperance, but these latter never bear any of the marks of it until they become acquainted with civilised man. The kava-root and other narcotics produce a stupefaction, but they leave no blotches, no laxity of muscle, no disgusting redness of the eyes, and all the wretched symptoms induced by spirits.

Leaving Terceira on 10 June 1831, we next arrived at Cadiz. The harbour is noble, the city one of the finest in Spain and, if properly garrisoned, must be capable of sustaining an obstinate defence. I make these observations, begging the reader to understand that I think I now know a good deal about the subject of defence, having heard an almost perpetual conversation about the capability of defence of one place or another in parts of the world where there were no guns or castles, as well as in those which were strongly fortified.

Cadiz, founded by the Phoenicians, has anchored the proud navies of Spain in every age of Spanish greatness, from Columbus to the gathering of the invincible Armada, to Villeneuve's sailing to be beaten at Trafalgar. The Earl of Essex, the favourite of Queen Elizabeth, took this city with his troops in 1596, burning it before leaving with their booty. It then sustained several English and French sieges during the Napoleonic wars. It is an old city, full of those things that interest a traveller whose views are directed to objects less superficial than those which strike the eye of the common observer. Our tastes change with our experience. First we look at whatever stands most prominent – buildings and people – but we afterward direct our attention to more minute matters, which do not lie on the surface, in all probability finding more satisfaction in these researches than in gazing at what everybody sees.

But I am deprived of the pleasure of describing this city fully, as we were not permitted to stay there. This was at first surprising to me, for I could not conceive of any cause why I should not see the people of Cadiz, especially as I had informed my female friends at Manila that I was to visit Cadiz, and therefore was under various commands from them to some of their friends in the city. But it was Manila that was the cause of our problem, when it became known we had departed from there when the cholera had been rife. Our logs, also, showed that two of our men had died of this disorder. The Cadiz authorities now became very peremptory, threatening to fire on us if we did not depart instantly. This we found silly and arbitrary, and how ridiculous these quarantine laws seemed to us, who had been out of danger over a distance of fifteen thousand miles of ocean! So, not having a single man sick of anything except accidental indisposition, we were forced to leave this port without discharging a particle of cargo, and to direct our course to Bordeaux.

This disease did not then appear in my eyes as it since has. I considered it entirely an Asiatic disorder, and one that would be confined to those countries. It had, I thought, passed from the River Hoogly and the Ganges to Manila, where I knew it to be fatal among the lower classes of society, although by no means confined to them. Still, the higher classes in Manila thought so little of it or, rather, said so little about it that I did not think much of its deadliness. And, as I have commented, only two of our sailors died, and their deaths by this disease made no very deep impression on my mind. It was only after we were denied the hospitalities of Christians at Cadiz, I began to reflect on the selfishness of people in their fear of an epidemic. I was also aware that this sweeping disorder had entered Europe at times and been very deadly.

But little did I think it would ever spread over my own dear country, causing so great a panic that for nearly a mile in the principal street of New York, at noonday, not half a dozen people could be seen. Desolation extended over all my native city, and while even now, preparing my journal for publication, every hour the house is filled with bulletins of the progress of this mighty scourge of mankind, the different symptoms, and the different treatments being put forward distracting every one. It was difficult to know what course to pursue when a person was attacked and until the disease was far advanced it was almost impossible to tell if the patient was sick with it or not, the symptoms being almost as various as the patients, cramps, diarrhoea, and occasional spasms are general premonitions, but no headache or dizziness marks its coming on. Rather like the apoplexy, its forerunner is a high state of animal spirits, before it strikes like a thief in the night. I never left New York during the whole time it was raging in the city, and had an opportunity of witnessing its disorganising effects on society, as well as the sufferings of those whom it attacked.

But the disease, and even the deaths, were nothing to the alarm that spread through all circles, and seemed to be a disease of itself – and even more malignant than the cholera. The constituted authorities did much, and the rich subscribed large sums of money, but if individuals in common life had not made exertions, personal and pecuniary, the sufferings would have been far more intense.

Such sweeping calamities can have a sad effect on the human mind, drying up the generous currents of the heart, and destroying all wholesome ceremonies of burial and funeral honours. Although there are frequently unnecessary expenses attending a funeral, yet there is something dreadful in having a friend die in such a manner as to see them hurried to the grave as one might see a vile suicide so treated. To see a loved being in health one hour, sick the next, dead the next, and then despatched to the grave before his ashes are cold is too much for human nature. I believe if everyone was obliged to live in the city during the rage of the sickness, many evils would be avoided. The natural ties between the rich and the poor and the middle classes of society would not lie sundered, one could give relief to others, and all, depending on Heaven, would go on as usual in most things. The great evil of this disease is that fear slays more than disease itself. In future days, the folly of flying from the cholera will be evident to all, and the great mass of inhabitants come to the truth that 'I ran from trouble, and trouble ran and overtook me.'

All the individual miseries which have flowed from the cholera will never be known. The tears and prayers of widows and orphans may have their influence with the God of mercies, and another scourge may not, perhaps, overtake them. This disease has touched the rich, but it has dwelt with the poor. It does, indeed, sweep off vice, but does not only inflict the vicious. The temperate, the abstemious, the cautious, and even the extremely scrupulous fall victims to its ravages. 'Be ye ready' is a maxim for all who live among men.

9. Bordeaux. History and description. Delight at seeing the flag of our country. Visit to the tomb of Montesquieu. Sketch of the Archbishop of Bordeaux, his residence in America and his popularity there. Reception of a file of American newspapers. American books and their value on ships. Farewell to Bordeaux.

ON 20 JUNE 1831 we arrived at Bordeaux (long 0° 34' W/lat 44° 50' 13" N), which is the chief city of the department of the Gironde. It is built on the left bank of the river Garonne, that is, the left bank after military language. This, I discovered, is different from naval usage, as military men speak of 'going down' a river, and naval men as 'sailing up'. In consideration of the loyalty of this city, Louis XVIII built a fine bridge across the Garonne, this structure having seventeen arches and being seven hundred feet in length. This was the first time I ever had an opportunity of visiting what might be called an ancient city. Those I had seen did not exceed three hundred years in age: this was founded so early that there is no record of its precise age. It was known to the Romans in the days of Caesar, and in the fifth century it was taken by the Goths in their sweeping march of destruction. It was destroyed after this by the Normans, but being a very convenient place for commerce, it soon rose again as an important city. It came into the hands of Louis VII by his marriage with the daughter of the Duke of Guyenne. The king was soon divorced from his wife, but she retained the city. In 1152 she married the Duke of Normandy, who afterward became King of England. The antiquarians here pretend to show the precise spot where the King of France (when made prisoner by the Black Prince) was confined for more than ten years. A few years after, the memorable feats of the Maid of Orleans saw the city restored to France. About a century after this, it was nearly destroyed by a rebellion of the people on account of some arbitrary taxation upon salt, an article much used here for preserving provisions for vessels. A place of great commercial consequence to France, it was protected by the Bourbons, and in gratitude remained loyalist during the Revolution of 1789, for which it was severely punished by furious republicans. It was the last place to yield to the revolutionists, and the first to hail the restoration of the Bourbons.

The city has all the marks of antiquity, some of the masonry and walls being probably laid before the Christian era. To an American, these walls, in which there are set nineteen gates, give the place a heavy appearance. Everything about the city looks as though in former days the inhabitants were capable of making a formidable resistance, particularly before the invention of gunpowder. In the suburbs, however, there are delightful residences.

The number of inhabitants is not exceeding one hundred thousand, nearly all Catholics. There are forty-six Catholic churches, and but one Protestant. Some of the former are noble edifices, though not all are in the best repair. Bonaparte built a palace here about the time of his Austrian alliance, perhaps more to conciliate the people, rather than with the intent of residing here any considerable time. He wished to eradicate from the people all affection for the Bourbons, and one way was to display the munificence of his new government. This was not bad policy, but proved of no avail. The attempts he made to benefit France, and they were not a few, were all destroyed by his Spanish and Russian wars – where he was beaten by the elements as well as men.

The harbour at Bordeaux is well protected by forts, and looks much more lively than the city does, the most cheerful sight to me being all the American flags flying from the shipping, more frequently than of any other nation but France. To one who had been long from home, it sent a summer feeling to my heart. Long respected for the enterprise of our merchants, and for the glory of our victories, our flag has not only been consecrated by bravery, but commemorated by the muse. And as I saw it waving from the tall masts of our noble vessels, I could not refrain from repeating the closing lines of one of the poets of my native city, lines written while the war fever was upon us.

For ever float that standard sheet!
Where breathes the foe that stands before us,
With freedom's soil beneath our feet,
And freedom's banner streaming o'er us!

The American Flag, Joseph Rodman Drake (1795–1820)

There is also a whale fishery carried on here, but the commanders of these whale ships are mostly Americans, as in fact are the seamen. An American whale ship is a little empire, generally one of the best regulated ones. Every one has a share in the profits, which works wonders. No people are more hardy than whalemen, and none have been more prosperous in their business. I was sorry to hear that the sand was accumulating at the mouth of this harbour, but as human ingenuity is now busy to find out some remedy for such evils, I trust the problem will be one of no great continuance.

The Bordeaux museum is large, but did not abound with as many curiosities as I expected, although the library of the Academy of Sciences was the largest I had ever seen. There were some splendid editions, but not many in comparison with the whole number of volumes. The academy of the deaf and dumb has good repute, but I had no opportunity of seeing a display of the pupils. In every part of the city there is something of the bustle of business, but more particularly at the gates opening towards the river. But these are not much visited by ladies.

I went to the church of St Bernard to see the tomb of Montesquieu, who was born in the neighbourhood of this city, and buried here. The French have a great reverence for his memory, and from the enthusiasm with which they speak of him, one would think he was some Lord Byron, or Thomas Moore, who had written poetry until every lady's head was turned with it. In this case, my companions could not tell me anything he had written, but only that every Frenchman admired it! At length I found an English copy of his *Spirit of the Laws*. From this, as far as I could judge, he seems to deserve the reputation of a great man, but I still wonder how he came to be admired by the French ladies, except perhaps it is a fashion among them to admire great men. I wish this was the fashion in our own country, but I fear that thousands of our New York ladies pass by Trinity Churchyard in Broadway without knowing that a greater man than Montesquieu has a monument there, the monument of one of whom it might be said:

When, certain death to honour and to trade,
A sponge was talked of as our only aid,

That to be saved we must be more undone,
And pay off all our debts by paying none,
Our Country's better genius, born to bless
And snatch our sinking credit from distress,
Didst thou step forth, and, without sail or oar,
Pilot the shattered vessel safe to shore.

'The Candidate', Charles Churchill (1731–64)

The present Archbishop of Bordeaux, John Cheverus, was for many years an inhabitant of the United States. During the reign of terror in 1793, being then a young Catholic priest, he fled to England, and from there to Boston in company with the Rev Dr Matignon. In Boston, these two priests did much good, and when a Catholic Bishop of Boston became necessary, Matignon urged that his young friend should be appointed, rather than himself. As bishop, Cheverus became the most popular man in that city among all denominations, on good terms with every sect of Christians: polite, affable, and kind, his labour unceasing whether among the rich or poor. Probably no man ever lived in Boston more generally beloved. After twenty-seven years' labour in the United States, he was appointed by Louis XVIII Bishop of Montauban, and requested to leave the United States as soon as possible. At first he declined the appointment, preferring to live in his own humble way in Boston, rather than change it for the parade of a French bishop's life. But the request being repeated, it is said, by the king himself, he left America for France, separating painfully from his old flock.

When he reached Montauban, the Protestants vied with the Catholics to do him honour, while he was always ready to do all any service that lay within his power. A great storm caused the rivers near Montauban to overflow their banks and endanger the lives of the farmers. Calling together all the active spirits of the city, Bishop Cheverus led the way in a very small boat to assist those in jeopardy. He brought hundreds back to the city, opened his palace, and lodged and fed them until the waters had abated, and did the same for cattle and other property. The king, hearing of this, and knowing that his finances were not in a very flourishing condition, sent him a considerable sum of money, all of which he distributed among those who had suffered most. So when the old Archbishop of Bordeaux died he was appointed, by universal acclamation, to fill his place. At Bordeaux, he was made by Charles X a peer of France. This office was not given to him because he wished it, but the king thought he would bring a share of good influence to the Chamber of Peers. It is also said he refused the office of becoming tutor to the young Duke of Bordeaux, heir-apparent to the throne, this post being considered in France the highest honour that could be given to any subject – that of forming the mind of him who was to reign – and thereby, in some measure, reigning himself.

It could be plainly seen when we were there that there was a gloom on the face of the good bishop, for he could not be ignorant of the state of the public mind in Paris, with some symptoms of a revolution appearing even in the loyal city of Bordeaux. A few days after our departure the revolution broke out in Paris which hurled Charles from the throne, and called in a 'citizen king'. In this change of affairs, the bishop lost his peerage, but this caused no grief to the good man, now being able to devote his whole time to ecclesiastical duties. It would have been fortunate for the young duke if he had had such a guardian and instructor as Bishop Cheverus. For if Charles X had been instructed by a wise, prudent teacher as to the nature and feelings of men, he would not have lost his crown. But I believe Cheverus never took an active part as a politician, his whole soul was in his religious duties. Like Fenelon, he only wished to do good.

France is a delightful country, and under a mild government would be a happy one. Everybody strives to be as happy as they can in France. It is not always so with us, as among some of our people there is a disposition to look on the dark side. If we hear of the approach of a comet, it disturbs the minds of some who are not wanting in good sense in other things, but the approach of a comet in France would produce pleasant sensations, with people only envying the scientific the pleasure they would find in watching its progress through the heavens. There is also a great ease of manners in the French, habitual politeness, and such a desire to make you happy, that one is unwilling to leave.

French agriculture, it is said, is in a prosperous state. There is a neatness about their fields and vineyards that is delightful to one accustomed to a ruder culture. The cultivators of the soil own much more of it than they did before the Revolution. It seemed to me almost impossible that this could be a people that only a few years ago in the age of a nation saw fathers, sons, and brothers fall by the dagger of the assassin, or under the bloody guillotine. There are no traces of those miseries now – unless, now and then, the mark of a cannonball on some old house. From reading all the agonising details of the Revolution, I expected to find many insane wretches, but all my inquiries, and I made them until they created a smile, could not produce a single maniac whose madness could be traced to witnessing, or sharing, these horrors. How soon a generation is forgotten! Even Napoleon, whose name was on every tongue from one end of the earth to the other, was now seldom mentioned anywhere in France. A lesson to those who seek fame though devastation and blood!

In Bordeaux I found a file of American newspapers. Nothing in them new or interesting but to me as dear as the light that visits my eyes: little squabbles of editors, complaints of neglected actors, the purls required to vend patent medicines, or call attention to a sale of the last importation of bonnets or fans. The whole medley was delightful. I could rejoice at the wedding register, and drop a tear over the obituary notices. The exile never kissed the ground on his return to his native land with more enthusiasm than I read these newspapers, some only fifty days old. After three years, they seemed to me as thrown on the breakfast table wet from the press, while such were the new publications I saw advertised, that while I was absent, all my countrymen had been busy cultivating their minds, and I expected to find every one so improved that I should hardly dare to see my old friends.

I also picked up some American books of recent date and read with delight. I made no criticisms, for one long absent from home never complains of anything from that quarter. I wish that all who criticise their own people were obliged to wait before they commenced their reviews until they had got three or four thousand miles from home. Any writer of distinction seeing his works in distant countries must be happy indeed. Irving, Cooper, Webster, and several of our poets were found at many places we visited, and those and other American names were familiar in Asia and Africa, as well as in Europe. English vessels are more likely to bring out recent literary and scientific productions, but they do not equal us in a general and useful library made up for a voyage. Hardly a single American vessel thinks of putting to sea without taking several hundred volumes, master mariners having found out that officers and men on a long voyage can both do their duties, and improve their minds. The selection is often not the best that might be made, and it would be a service if someone acquainted with books were to make out a catalogue of such as should be collected for 'ordinary', and for 'long', voyages. All the approved naval journals and collections of voyages, are indispensable, of course, plus good commercial dictionaries, while geographies and gazetteers should be always at hand. Nor should works of taste be forgotten: an interesting work carries double charms on shipboard. The mind is then concentrated, and cannot be dissipated by amusements or trifles, plus any moral lesson sinks in deeper where there is no distraction.

Our great mathematician, Dr Bowditch (although considered greater in Europe than in America), performed many long voyages from the United States to India, and always having with him good officers, had leisure to go through those long and difficult calculations which have since laid the foundation of his fame. Every person at sea is constantly reminded of him, as his *Navigator* is on every officer's table. It is said, also, that the numerous corrections made in tables by him were done at sea. I am surprised that tales or poetry are not often written at sea, for passengers surely have leisure when officers have no spare time, the inspiration coming, generally, from the pure air, which after all may be the best inspiring agent in nature. The dreams of Delphos were upon some divine afflatus, as the poets call it, which was probably nothing more than a sweet bracing wind.

I was to learn in France that my countrymen were much respected, and we were no longer considered an infant nation but one that bore a proud flag, and was rearing historians, poets, orators, and above all a class of profound statesmen. And I looked forward to the day when my own dear boy might be an active man among them. But this prospective view, generally long to those who have children, did not seem to me half so long as I had been absent from my child.

Travellers, it is said, are mostly short lived, and I can easily conceive of the truth of the remark, for they suffer and enjoy so much that the human frame is exhausted by their various excited emotions – anxiety, good news, bad news – all the changes that agitate the heart. And though I longed to sit down once more in my own chamber, and enjoy, oh, sweetly enjoy, all my former domestic quiet, yet I would not give up the memory of the things I have seen and suffered to be ensured of the most protracted existence. Such contradictions we are, and such we shall always remain.

The distance from home seemed now a mere trifle, three thousand miles. And that across the Atlantic, my own ocean, which I did not think now would be deceitful, since I had braved so many dangers in the southern Pacific.

When the anchor was weighed for our departure, and our friends came to take leave, I thought only of a pleasant sail home as on a party of pleasure. The countenances of the hardy seamen, too, now seemed to glow with the thoughts of their native land as, seemingly without an order, they sprang to their duties.

10. Conchology – the 'eyestone' shell and its claim to animate life. The Flying Dutchman and the superstitions of sailors. Causes of their ignorance and the neglect of their education. Happiness of seamen on United States ship *Vincennes* at Manila. Manner in which seamen should be treated.

WHEN YOUNG, I had received from seafaring connections a pretty collection of shells and now, on the voyage to New York from Bordeaux, I took the opportunity to arrange those I had collected in the South Pacific from the beaches of the many islands we had visited, my passion for conchology increasing when I learned from writings on the subject how long this branch of natural history had attracted the attention of mankind, and how much had been done regarding classification and description. I had never dreamed that such as the philosophers of Greece had paid attention to picking and describing shells, and that more than two thousand years ago Aristotle made a treatise upon conchology for the benefit of his pupil, Alexander the Great. At first it seemed strange to me that he who was deep in the mysteries of logic could stoop to examine shells, or that he who was grasping at universal empire could listen to a discourse on them. But I now believe that the more intelligent an age and nation, the more these minute subjects are attended to. Even though during the night of darkness, when the world was overrun with super-stition, no attention was paid to these works of God as displayed in his creation and providence. However, it is little more than half a century since conchology was revived, and is now in train to become extensively understood, the admirable construction of shells for their intended purposes, and their beautifully variegated colours surely affording proof that the superintending hand of Providence extends to even to the minutest objects of creation.

It is a beautiful sight to look along the shores of some of the islands near the equator and mark the endless variety of shells, houses of tenants long since dead, and now thrown up by winds and waves. If we could but rake the bottom of the seas we would find specimens much more beautiful. The shells that the pearl-divers brought up to us with their inhabitant alive had tints far more exquisite than those bleached by the sun and rains, and washed by ten thousand tides. The pearl oyster, as the conch is called which contains the pearl, is particularly worthy of examination. It is about three or four times as large as the common oyster, and, as far as I could learn, has power of locomotion to find his food. The shell is called mother-of-pearl, even if no pearls are found within the shell. The pearl was long supposed to be fixed to the shell, to assist in opening it, or for some other purpose, heaven only knows what! The pearl, however, grows under the most fleshy parts of the oyster. This creation, like that of ambergris, has never been satisfactorily accounted for, and perhaps never will. Perhaps the great Author of nature intended that the beings he endowed with reason should have perpetual enigmas to solve, so they could never reach him by attempting to fathom the secrets of nature, for he knows their ambition and their pride.

The natives of the South Seas use these shells in forming instruments such as hatchets, spears, fish-hooks, and knives, and if not equal to iron and steel they are vastly superior to silver or gold. To us on land, it is a little singular that the ancients attributed to the sea so many of the loveliest of their mythological creations: Venus arising from the foam, while Tritons sounded their shells; Cleopatra, who I read dissolved a most valuable pearl in vinegar, and drank it. The vinegar must have been stronger than that which we had, for I tried the same thing, and could not dissolve it in a whole day. A royal stomach indeed!

Then the nautilus, of which we gathered a great variety: quite a curiosity, and which has held a high rank in conchology for many reasons. It is a vessel, which some poets, ancient and modern, make the prototype of vessels and of sailing. Found in most warm countries, they are from the size of your thumbnail to upwards of eighteen inches from stem to stern – as sailors speak. The living part of the nautilus does not weigh much more than an ounce, whereas the shell would hold a quart. But the living part has the power of throwing all the water from the shell, and of sailing by projecting a membrane, which the sailors call its 'stern-sheet'. The outside of the shell is white and smooth, the inside of a pearly cast. The natives polish and ornament them, and use them as drinking cups. I have several bearing fancy sketches, and find these decidedly superior to most ladies' ornamental work, and to the patterns found on fashionable handkerchiefs or vandykes.[15]

The large shell generally called by the name of conch is found in the islands in great abundance. These are artificially perforated near the top, and used as the war trumpet by the natives. They are never sounded except as a general signal for muster. Their power is vastly greater than that of the trumpet, and they may be heard farther than any other martial instrument. Again, the ancients had the Triton, acting as trumpeter to Neptune, blow this shell. The ancients also considered these shells as carrying within them a spirit of echo, and whoever puts one of them to his ear will discover from whence that impression arose. There is a sound of distant waters in his ear: the lashing of the billows upon the beach. This shell, the conch, was brought to our country very early. I have been informed that some of the original settlers used them to call workmen to their meals. History also informs us that the Indians in the wars of King Philip were frightened from their purpose by the sound of this dinner-summoning conch. At a later period they were used to call the inmates of colleges to dinner or prayers.

There is, finally, a little shell called the 'eyestone'. I have seen no account of its classical name, though I do not say that there is none extant. A former impression of the powers of this shell was that it was gifted with life, but would sleep quiet until man wanted its services. This happened when a mote of dust, or other matter, got into someone's eye, At this, the eyestone was plunged into vinegar and revivified. It was then put into the sufferer's eye, where it was said to move round under the lid by natural action. Being so smooth, its excrescences all being destroyed by the vinegar acid, it gave no pain and, working under the lid, would push before it any speck of foreign matter, and relieve the eye in a short time. The science of the present day, however, is not content to receive anything on trust, and the notion of the vitality of the eyestone is now exploded like many other sailors' superstitions.

Sailors are superstitious because, simply, they are

ignorant and uneducated. Constantly seeing remarkable things, without being able by any knowledge they have to account for them, instead they recourse to their imaginations, these in turn leading them into many fallacies. Take the story of the Flying Dutchman, a ship said to haunt the seas off the Cape of Good Hope, so punished because its crew were wicked enough to deny the Christian religion, and to trample the cross under their feet for gain. For this unpardonable sin, this vessel and its crew were doomed to fly from place to place until the world should be destroyed.

Nineteen-twentieths of the sailors who double the Cape of Good Hope believe in the truth of the Flying Dutchman. They quote stories of other honest seamen who bear testimony to having seen this ship, and if solemn testimony was the only way to establish the truth of a matter, the existence of the Flying Dutchman would be as well supported as any event in history.

Cotton Mather speaks of a phantom-ship which appeared near the harbour of Boston – a vessel so long overdue she had been given up for lost, but was then seen by the Bostonians coming in swimmingly, under full sail, with men on her decks, then after an hour or two instantly vanishing never to be seen or heard of any more. For nearly two centuries this story was told to the belief of many (and the amusement of others), when an explanation was given by a similar appearance off New York. In 1826 the appearance of several vessels was seen from the Battery upon the horizon, clearly and distinctly, when the ships whose images were reflected were not within sight; these images by refraction were thrown upon a cloud, and now the natural philosophers explained a satisfactory solution to Cotton Mather's story. And there can be no doubt that in those seas where the Flying Dutchman has been again and again seen, that this effect is reducible to the same cause.

This story, just one of many superstitions held by seaman, makes it all the more astonishing that attempts to educate and reform our sailors should have been left so late. But ever since maritime commerce was introduced into the world, opinion has been that those who went down to the sea in ships should be rough, bold, and uncivil, even though moderns have now decided these characteristics do not necessarily make a good sailor. That they should be fearless arises from their duties; cowardice in them would lead to destruction, and they know it. Therefore, while they are very hardy from exercise and sea air, habit makes them often do an act whose consequences they do not stop to calculate, while profanity is more a degrading habit rather than a blasphemous disposition, often imitated from their officers.

Seamen's hearts, however, are usually right: generous and faithful – with even their prejudices usually on the side of virtue. So why, then, is the sailor deliberately left in ignorance? This subject is now of great importance, considering the great number of American sailors. For taking the navy, those engaged in foreign and domestic commerce, and the fisheries, there cannot be less than sixty thousand: forty-three thousand in commerce, ten thousand in the navy, seven thousand in the fisheries. Instruction might be given to, certainly, the first two groups, at an easy and cheap rate, to make them more respectable citizens without injuring them as sailors.

The fault is with those who employ and control the sailor. Merchants will say, reasoning like despots: 'My authority is at an end when they know anything more than mere seamanship, if they can navigate, they would take my ship and go where they please with her. Enlighten these men, now only good machines to work or fight a ship, and make them understand their situation, you raise at once the price of wages, and commerce can not afford this.' But wages are always incorporated with other expenses on a cargo, and the consumer, not the merchant, pays for them. But with education would not the regularity of the conduct of seamen lessen insurance, and produce quicker voyages, and therefore, in the end, favour the merchant? If sailors were educated and kept sober, there would be less chance of their turning pirate, and committing those crimes at which all mankind shudder, and which are now so prevalent that scarcely a paper is issued without some mention of loss of lives and property by piracy. Humanity calls upon our naval forces to avenge the injuries. But instruction in science and moral discipline would, in most instances, prevent them.

Is it not extraordinary that there is no system of instruction for sailors, except such as is left to the discretion of masters of vessels? There are in the world at least a million seamen fighting their country's battles, or assisting in its commerce – and hardly a school to serve them.

No farmer hires a man who is not recommended to him as able-bodied, and well acquainted with his duties. Yet a merchant fixes upon his voyage, selects his master, gets his vessel loaded and fit for sea, and only *then* drums up his crew, only asking if a man be a 'good seaman', without taking any account of the moral character of the sailor they employ – whether the man is a pirate or an honest seaman. And as long as there are so many bad men who resort to the seas, perhaps to escape the punishment due to their crimes on land, no wonder that so many deeds of horror are perpetrated once out of sight of that land. Inquiry should be made into every man's character before he ships, and then proper arrangements made to treat him well on the voyage as to food and instruction.

As for the carrying of spirits and liquors, the allowance of whisky should be cut off by fair contract, and something substituted in its place. Government should not save by any of these regulations, but should rather 'over' than 'under' pay, let good and wholesome meals be always provided, and good and wholesome instruction be constantly going on, and the seamen would be content, and the ship forever secure.

However, I believe some good works have been begun in many of the seaport towns in this country. Provision has been made for mariners' churches, and (no doubt with some fanaticism) much good has been done in many respects, while in the navy there are now chaplains who can both preach and pray. I would not have a ship a conventicle, but much may be done without cant or overstrained piety. Get men thinking right – you will find them acting well.

An example was put before us in Manila. Just before we arrived, the United States sloop-of-war *Vincennes* had visited there: in all respects, a fine ship. The people of Manila spoke of her neatness, order, and the decorum of her crew. This was owing to the honourable agreement between the captain and the chaplain. They understood each other, and the crew understood both. Both these officers were men of sense, and expected no more than could be performed by men, but still took every measure to bring to the minds of the crew a just sense of reasoning, moral instruction going on while duty was performed. No ship ever yet went round the world with so much ease, with so little loss of human life, and with so much harmony, as the *Vincennes*. Though an ordinary voyage to them, it was an extraordinary voyage to every looker-on, the discipline of the crew being a source of wonder at every place they visited. Yet the true Christian will always fight like a lion. It has never been found that principle destroys mental energy, but on the contrary sustains it through every contest. Change the moral character of your seamen: you will make them invincible. It is my belief that a crew of men formed on Christian precepts would not flinch from twice their number on what are commonly called 'the floating hells'. I am not one of those fanatics who think that all seamen can be made Christians, but from what I have seen I believe that every crew can be made a well-regulated family, with the sort of decency and decorum that may prevail on shore. That vice can be rooted out of the world, I am not so weak as to suppose, but I do believe sailors can be made as good men as others

The Bishop of Cloyne wrote 'Westward the star of Empire takes its way.' And if man in America is to rise to a higher eminence as an intelligent being than he ever did in the Old World, it will be from a disposition to benefit his species.

Man is enfeebled by vice, but the frenzy of inebriation may last for only a few moments, while calm determination and a clear view is worth more than all the fury of accidental excitement. I know there are honest men who will think these reasonings a species of fanaticism, and I have no doubt some things said at the Bethels and mariners' churches may savour of fanaticism, but that is no argument against attempts to make sailors rational, moral, and religious beings. It never was, and never will be, the case that a reform can be conducted in all respects by the cool dictates of the understanding.

How to effect this? In the first place, I would introduce on board a few well-written anecdotes of Christian mariners: works, however, without sectarianism. Also epitomes of the best voyages – accounts that will make the profession appear in its true and honourable light. By other small treatises, the sailor should also have explained to him his duties. If these were clearly laid down, he would learn them in half the time as it takes by curses and floggings. He should also be offered instruction in science and navigation. This may seem chimerical to one who owns several ships, and wishes to get them navigated as cheap as possible, but commercial calculation should yield to general interest and common understanding.

As for myself, a woman, offering these suggestions: when there were but three or four banks in the United States, the stockholders, it is said, objected to having any more, as the mysteries of managing them were above ordinary comprehension. Equally, it may be said the managing of the moral and temporal condition of sailors may be thought to be above the comprehension of a woman but, however, one thing is certain, that if my remarks are of no service, they are at least harmless.

To ship a sailor, learn him to do his duty, and to bring him back safe after he has honourably discharged it, has no mystery, but a good deal of common sense. These same merchants' stockholders, it may be noted, are making ample provision to preserve the morals and enlighten the minds of their clerks to prevent fraud and peculation. Why should not equal attention be paid to the moral and intellectual improvement of mariners?

A plan has lately been suggested by a patriotic and intelligent member of Congress to make the whole army of the United States one great seminary of instruction, and to dismiss all its idle and good-for-nothing drones, and introduce youthful ambition in their place. The plan will succeed when it is properly understood, at which time the army will become much more efficient, and thousands of good citizens on their discharge from military duties will be added to the republic. So with sailors, when, either disabled or disinclined to follow their profession, they may be enabled to fill other some station in society if sufficiently educated. But with the present system, when a sailor can no longer discharge his shipboard duties, he is considered an outcast, and usually left to expire in some asylum of charity, or die by intemperance. This is wrong. And the moralists and philanthropists should set about devising its remedy – and the sooner the better.

11. Observations on the progress of discovery among maritime races of the world. Remarks on the marine of various nations. The aurora borealis. Anecdote of its appearance early in the last century.

THE GLORIES OF discovery are divided among the maritime nations of Europe, and our own country. First came those who sailed from the Gulf of Finland, though not yet known as having any navy, or vessels of commerce. Then the Portuguese and Spaniards, hardly known now in the countries over which their nations once held sway. The treasure galleons which once sailed from Manila to South America, and to the Iberian Peninsula, are now only reminiscences of history, and it requires some degree of faith to believe they ever existed, while Venice, Genoa, and Florence are as if they had never been. The only flags now are those of England, France, Russia, the United States, and now and then the kingdom of the Netherlands, as the commerce of Holland is reviving.

The autocrat of all the Russias has evinced a desire

that his empire should be ranked among the naval nations of the world, and has been at some expense to support this assumption, and while his share in the bloody battle of Navarino has done him little honour, the voyage of Von Kotzebue has. Russia has too deep an interest in the western Pacific not to have a respectable force on its northeast coast, while the opening up of the Black Sea will give Russia facilities for commerce and for increasing her navy, which she has never before possessed. Russia is slowly but surely extending her powers over every sea and her maritime power is one that will increase, if not rapidly, yet surely. The spirit of Peter the Great is in existence in that government, and will not easily be driven out of it. He has said, in pride of valour, 'Nature has but one Russia, and it shall have no rival.' But at that time he hardly knew that an empire had been planted in this western world; our republic which now bids fair to share the honours of international influence with Russia.

France has not extended her empire much since the battles of the Nile and Trafalgar, but is steadily increasing her marine. Her navy now falls little shorter in point of numbers than that of Great Britain, while her colonies are next to the British in fertility and commerce. France has always determined in modern times to have her share in exploring and in governing the world. Since her disasters in the great battles with England she has been able to put forward less than her former display, yet, I have no doubt, she has lost nothing of her pride, sagacity, or world enterprise. For although there is no parade made about it, we find French ships everywhere, pursuing their course in silent duty, but not without gaining information. If France is suffered to remain in peace, we may rely upon it she will have no humble views of her knowledge and her power.

But while French discoveries are only partially given to the world, the discoveries of England are made public at once. England, it is true, considers the oceans as her own, and sails them as if this superiority will never be disputed. The imposing appearance of her ships impresses the people in every distant region they visited with an idea of the power and importance of her empire, especially when contrasted with the smaller and inferior equipment of other European nations. Native peoples possess no other means of judging of the relative importance of the countries which traded with them, except by size and armament, and no endeavours are spared by those who navigate British vessels to reinforce this favourable impression. From this, every expression of admiration and reverence that aborigines have at their command has been exhausted on the British navy. This influence is fairly earned, however inimical it may be to other nations. And I know not how they can remedy the evil which is experienced by the superiority of England, except by emulating that country's commercial exertions.

The United States, if her commerce and marine increase as they have done for twenty years past, will hopefully in twenty years to come be as much involved in the trade of the southern hemisphere as England is now. The visits of our vessels of war to the remote parts of the western and eastern Pacific have had a good effect on the minds of the Indians, Malays, and Chinese, who think nothing of justice, but only as it may be enforced by power. In time, some civilised nations must be masters of these remote islands, and it would be well for us to have our share. Settlements on some lately discovered islands would serve both whaling ships and other vessels, and would create new markets for our articles of commerce.

The naval character of the people of the United States may be said almost to be incorporated with, and form a part of, their nature. Our forefathers began to navigate the ocean almost as soon as they had landed on these shores. A hundred years later the colonies had a spirited little navy that carried the provisions and troops in 1717 to Canada. By the time of the war of 1745 our power was respectable, and vessels of considerable size were sent to the siege of Louisburg. In the war of 1755, and onward to 1763, American sailors were distinguished for enterprise and bravery. In that of 1775, the colonies astonished the English by the number and spirit of their privately armed vessels, and Congress created a considerable marine in a very short time. The national and private armed ships, if our histories are correct, took from the enemy fifteen hundred vessels, and left many heroes as yet to be celebrated by our biographers. I may be thought overenthusiastic, but the achievements of those who won for us the high and proud name we now boast have taken deep hold of my mind. In 1798 the nation was awakened by the insult offered our flag by France, a navy was instantly built, and its value immediately realised. The orders under which our fleet sailed at first were so restricted that not much was done excepting by way of protection, but when these orders were enlarged they captured nearly a hundred vessels, and recaptured many which the French cruisers had taken from the United States, Captains Truxton, Little, Shaw, and others gaining an imperishable name. Our people had hoped that this little navy would be cherished, but the policy of that day dictated that all our ships, except a few frigates, were sold, a subject of great mortification to some merchants and friends of the navy. But the glory it had won was secured, and we had satisfied ourselves that our muscle and nerve were as good as any other nation.

But the fates were determined we should have no chance to grow rusty. Certain piratical powers, whose robberies and extortions had been borne long by the nations of Europe, expected that the commerce of a new and feeble nation (as they saw us) would be easy prey. The state of the times, it is true, made it necessary for us, for a time, to tamely purchase peace and immunity from Morocco and Algiers, pirates that had been the scourge of nations for a thousand years from the Pillars of Hercules to the furthest shores of the Mediterranean. This was galling to a free people, although to their everlasting disgrace Spain, Portugal, France, and England, with Denmark and Sweden, also paid tribute.

But although policy required we should suffer then in silence, we were not prepared to bear the yoke forever. In 1800 a ship commissioned to carry tribute to the Dey of Algiers was sent on by this savage in a most insulting manner to his master, the Grand Seignor at Constantinople. This indignity was submitted to in order to exempt our mariners from being taken as slaves, though the people of the United States called aloud to have these assassins punished. Then the Bey of Tunis raised his voice for tribute, while the Bashaw of Tripoli declared war with the United States, thinking to strike terror into us. Soon after this declaration, one of our oldest naval commanders was sent out with three frigates and a schooner. His instructions were that he was not to fight if he could help it, but this could not be avoided. In August 1801 Lieutenant Stewart in the *Enterprise* (12 guns) took a Tripolitan ship of war, the first we ever subdued. She had twenty killed, and thirty wounded, but there was not one American injured. Our naval tactics were now acknowledged to be of the first order.

In the spring of 1802 a squadron was sent out under the command of Captain R V Morris who, being charged with want of energy, was superseded by Preble, acompanied by Bainbridge, Decatur, Charles Morris, MacDonough, and others. These men and their ships blockaded Tripoli, while watching the movements of Algiers, Morocco, and Tunis, which like tigers were ready to start on their prey. The Emperor of Morocco eventually came to terms, and the Dey of Algiers was quiet, when Preble then determined to chastise Tripoli, using the force he had with him – a few Neapolitan gunboats – little better than mudscows. On 3 August 1804 he made the first attack. This caused the barbarian to lessen his demands of tribute, but his new terms were not admissible, and another attack was made on the 5th. On the 28th Preble attacked again, and also on 3 September. Peace was concluded the next summer between Tripoli and the United States on equitable terms. This event astounded all Europe, that a new power should have carried on a war with such slight means, and to so glorious a termination, while his Holiness the Pope believed it a miracle, and it was indeed bordering on the miraculous that a few ships of an infant country should instantly effect what powerful nations had unsuccessfully attempted. The wretches released from slavery sent their cries of joy abroad to echo throughout the world, while the corsairs who had formerly sailed these seas with the utmost insolence now fled from the first appearance of an American sloop-of-war as if it were a vessel of the largest class.

From this war to that of 1812 our navy was not much increased, nor extensively employed. Many were apprehensive that its character would be lost in peace, and many statesmen thought the United States could do without a navy. Then came the war of 1812, when the navy fought itself into fame and was most nobly improved by Jones, Lawrence, Perry, Chauncey, Stewart, Decatur, Blakeley, and so many others that it is almost invidious to mention names.

So now we have fifty vessels of war, nearly half of which are in commission, the whole being supported by less than three millions of dollars annually, while for this proud defence the population is not taxed twenty-five cents a head, the French cost being four times as great as ours, the British nine. To keep the peace of the world at the present time, there are about 550 vessels of war in commission. Our force is only a twentieth part of this yet we have a much larger proportion of the commerce of the world to protect. Why all these calculations? ask my fair readers. I answer that I have been for nearly two years on the high seas, have reflected much upon the subject, and have some confidence in my own view of it.

It is pleasant now to pass from such calculations as the phenomena of war to the phenomena of nature. One evening, on our homeward voyage, I was called by my brother to witness a brilliant aurora borealis. I had hoped in the southern latitudes to have seen an aurora australis, but perhaps we had not sailed sufficiently south. This 'northern light' now illumining the heavens was not a novelty, for I had observed it as a schoolgirl, but now I was capable of making a better habit of observation. The phenomenon itself seems to have been first recorded in North America in 1719, on 17 December, but the causes which produced it then and now must have existed from the creation of the world, and it is strange there is no record in the annals of the New World before.

Now, the sun had been down about an hour when a dark cloud fringed the horizon, two or three degrees above it. This cloud was edged with white, sometimes changing to a brilliant fire colour, then arrows of light would dart from the cloud and stream high in the heavens. Then the clouds would be seen above the light, and new lights would rise on the second band of darkness, converging to a point almost over our heads. The shapes of light were constantly changing: now resembling a volcano, now pyramids or burning cities, but only for an instant remaining the same.

Reverting to the earlier mention of superstitions, a good story is told of the influence of the aurora borealis on the minds of some of our own countrymen, not this time mariners. In the early part of the last century, a marriage had been agreed between the son of a merchant, and the daughter of a highly respectable landholder, to be celebrated on 1 January. The company, all connections and relations, was very numerous and in great glee. The sun set, and a most beautiful aurora borealis appeared with streams of fire being thrown to the zenith. Although all eyes were upon it, viewing it without fear, the father of the bride seemed distressed, and in the most solemn manner announced his determination to put off the wedding. This threw the whole company into consternation. The young couple looked disappointed, but said nothing for that was a period of parental severity. At length, the clergyman arrived, delayed by making some notes upon that same phenomenon. The determination of the old gentleman was communicated to him, of which he seemed to take no notice, but instead explained to all present as much as was then known by philosophers on the subject of the aurora. He then mentioned the benevolence of the Deity, and how this was probably His way of keeping the atmosphere in the frozen regions in a proper state for respiration by the inhabitants – at this time of year without the cheering rays of the blessed sun, and how the electricity agitated in this manner assisted the poor Laplanders to procure food; also how eclipses of the sun and moon – once thought to portend disasters – were now used to accurately measure time. The father listened with great attention, at length avowed his conviction of his error, and the marriage was celebrated as first announced. How much good a clergyman can do when he unites the wisdom of the serpent with the harmlessness of the dove.

12. Reflections on drawing near my native land. The fates of the aboriginal natives, Sunday and Monday. Difficulties women experience in gaining information. The value of commerce. The influence of women. Love of the ocean and farewell to it. Last thoughts for our sailors.

BEFORE I DESCRIBE my feeling on drawing near to my native land, I will once again mention Sunday and Monday, the two prisoners taken by my husband. Sunday was a native of importance, taken shortly before Monday. He is without doubt a chief among his tribe, for he led an attack upon us, and bore himself bravely. He is a stout, well-made man, of five feet eleven inches in height, weighs about two hundred pounds, and is remarkably strong and active. His strength is wonderful, no one on board possessing equal muscular power. He is supposed to be about thirty-five years of age. He is very tractable and soon learned many English words, enough to understand from my husband that he shall return to his native land as soon as circumstances will permit. He has more of the African cast of features than the inhabitants of most of the islands we visited. He states he had three wives, to which number his rank entitled him, being the son of a king, an old man who did not come out to battle. He seems to be open, generous, and willing to do anything he can for others: he is extremely anxious to return to his native island, and promises to make all there do right.

Monday came from another island, being picked up from the water after his canoe was destroyed by the cannon shot. He is about twenty-two years of age, five feet eight inches high, stout made, and quick in his movements, ingenious, and very imitative – rather sullen in temper, but never appearing vindictive. At first he seemed to wish to remain in ignorance, but after a while came to a better disposition. His countenance is that of a savage in every respect. He has the Indian high cheekbones and the dark humours of the eye. He is not of a strong constitution, seeming rather inclined to consumption, but how any being could have that complaint who was born and lived in the climate he did I cannot tell.

Perhaps the thoughts of being a prisoner preyed on his mind, and the sickness of his heart was taken for that of another kind. At times this savage would sit and look steadfastly upon the ocean towards, as he probably thought, the point from whence he came, for whole hours together. Every kindness was shown him, he ate what he pleased, and when. Nor was a blow ever given him, the sailors having strict orders not to disturb him nor his companion. He wandered about the deck, and showed at length some marks of interest in things around him. He soon became familiar with clothes, and fond of them.

I am far from the opinion that these people whom we call savages have the worst dispositions on earth. On the contrary, I believe that if their hearts could be reached by kindness, they could easily be brought to observe the rules and decencies of society. I state this for the encouragement of those who may hereafter become missionaries to these benighted parts of Earth. This very savage may, and I trust will, be an efficient instrument in opening a way for the labours of pious men sent to these regions. Besides the good it will do, will it not be a source of happiness to those engaged in such a cause! Is there not a disposition in every enterprising mind to erect some memorial which will endure beyond the time he may live? Do not these unknown regions afford an opportunity for virtuous distinction? To carry civilisation and Christianity to such remote parts of the earth would have given joy to the apostles themselves.

I never saw happier beings than the missionaries of New Zealand, even though far from friends and country, and the good of savages their only reward. I have often thought of their sincerity, who were not among the poor and destitute in their own country, but possessed the means to bear a respectable part in society. They labour year upon year for the cure of souls, thinking of no recompense this side of heaven. How sincere the faith that can support them in all this! It is almost equal to that expressed by St Paul, who could wish himself condemned for Christ's sake. I loved them for staying there, but did not dare ask my heart if I could join them, as I should have feared a worldly answer from myself. But, thank heaven, I can never be put to the test.

And now, within our own waters, I began to question myself as to what purpose I had spent my time during this long voyage. Had I acquired and treasured up all the knowledge that I might have done? I was not prepared by education or habits to make the most of the situation, but had the consoling reflection that I had never distrusted Providence, had never repined and, as far as I was able, cheered my husband in his many misfortunes. I felt myself a much graver matron than when I embarked, and believed I now had more rational opinions for the government of life. Although I suffered much, I enjoyed more, and laid up a stock to reflect and reason upon during my future days. I had left my child for what was a short time to him, but a long one to me, but thought I had learned enough to balance the pain of this absence against the attainment of that discretion a mother should have in rearing a child. It is by the kindness of heaven that mothers do as well as they do, for most of us in the early part have only the philosophy of the heart, rather than that of the head, to direct us.

It was not for any specific purpose that I became a voyager, but simply to be a companion to my husband. My feelings and reasonings were uncontrolled, and the views I initially took of things were those of an unlearned mind. Everything was rare and strange, and excited my curiosity. If I ever again contemplated such a voyage, I think I should be better prepared to bring home something more worthy of myself and my countrywomen. The great difficulty we women feel in collecting information is the want of order and classification of our thoughts, and we therefore labour much harder to arrive at true conclusions than those who have a regular pigeonhole in which to place information. Although I doubt whether any scientific observer would have had more thoughts than passed through my own teeming brain, he would have known how to arrange them and draw conclusions, while whatever observations or conclusions I might make were liable to be dispersed for not knowing where to preserve them. The unstudied and unpractised mind, however, observes many things that escape the notice of the best educated.

Every vessel we met I amused myself with con- sidering as a messenger to bring us some tidings from the friends we left at our departure, but they often passed at too great a distance to speak to them, and as it was a time of peace and the weather fair, we left each other with the pleasurable sensation that each was well provided with all necessaries. These sights thickened as we came nearer our own shores, affording new proofs of our country's advancing commercial enterprise

On arriving now at the termination of my voyage, and taking a retrospective view of what had principally fixed my attention, I felt my mind drawn back to the South Pacific. I hope one day to live to see the islands in this ocean inhabited by my countrymen, and under the protection of my country. There is, at present, no obstacle in the way of this. Settlements might be made on some of the islands we discovered, with every prospect of securing the commerce of those seas, or at least sharing it with other nations. Our country has only existed about two centuries, although only being acknowledged and received into the greater family of nations for about half a century, yet we are considered the third commercial people on the globe; at first carrying the commodities of other nations, but soon carrying our own.

The first step to be taken in order that all the benefits may be derived from the Pacific islands must be to spread the light of the Gospel and civilisation through the medium of missionaries. For this purpose, I hope I shall not call in vain on my countrywomen when I implore them to continue their exertions on behalf of the missions, not only as matters of charity, but also of disseminating knowledge. On both sides of the water we possess the requisite female capabilities: Hannah More, Miss Edgeworth, Mrs Hemans in England, and our own countrywomen Mrs Sigourney and Miss Sedgwick. And in those branches of which mathematics is the basis, Mrs Somerville has transcended all who have attempted previously to instruct youth, while another hundred others may be brought forward to prove what great work women do in advancing the social and intellectual condition of mankind.

The ocean itself I love to contemplate in its immensity, its sameness, its power, and as a medium of communication; all the attributes of sublimity, plus all the properties of usefulness – food for man and pathways for the world: 'And I have loved thee, Ocean!'

On 26 August we discovered land: my own, my native land. We were making fair progress towards it, but, notwithstanding, my impatience was such that I could have scolded the *Antarctic* for being so sluggish, even though I had during the whole voyage loved her as having carried me so safely. Approaching the harbour of New York, I could now compare it with others I had seen. What city in the world is so advantageously placed? Surrounded by rivers and washed by the sea, neither Europe, Asia, Africa, nor South America has anything to compare with it. Its deep waters, and its crowded marts of merchandise are unequalled anywhere in this country, and when we add the connection of the great inland lakes, there is no rival anywhere. In less than fifty years its population has increased tenfold. In 1783 it contained twenty thousand inhabitants, they now number more than two hundred thousand. And all seemed so busy and happy: a forest of masts appeared on either side of the city, closer together than the cedars of Lebanon. The time is fast coming, thought I, when this great city will rival all others of ancient or modern times.

On 27 August 1831 I came on shore. As I left our little bark, I could not help exclaiming to myself, 'Have I been almost two years in that schooner!' I had, and was as safe in her, I believe, as I should have been in a warship of seventy-four guns, if not altogether so comfortable. I stepped upon the soil of my native city and its spires, steamboats, bustle all seeming as I had left it apart from increase! In a few moments I embraced my child, my mother, my sisters, my friends, and was indeed greeted as one 'from a far country'. But on looking around, I saw the emblems of bereavement: my mother again a widow, my worthy stepfather having died of a consumption during my absence – a truly good man, who had been to me as an own father. A dear aunt, too, had paid the debt of nature. I mingled my tears with those of my surviving relatives, but who after so long an absence can expect to find home as it was left? But my mother and my child were alive and well, so I thanked heaven for what had been preserved, while sincerely mourning the departed.

New cares were soon allotted me, for in nine days after my return I was the happy mother of another fine son. Perhaps his mother's *Journal* may in some future day be read by him, and perhaps he may be stimulated to put some of her plans in train.

The public soon caught notice of our adventures; one of the seamen, Leonard Shaw, publishing his account of the massacre at the islands, our story was soon in every print. Business taking my husband to the south, I accompanied him. We were received with so much kindness and attention, and I had so many questions put to me for my version of the voyage, I determined to give this narrative to the public to indicate in part that little enterprise of mine – my voyage – has taught me what my sex can do if called to act in the business of life, and to show I now feel myself wedded to the seas as much as the Doge of Venice was to the Adriatic.

In life, I would ask no more than to learn reform was going on successfully to help the lot of the American sailor; in death, that the inscription on my tombstone declare that the ashes of the mariner's friend repose beneath it.

Notes

1. Dickinson, Emily, *Give Her This Day*, ed Louis Stiles Edgerly (Maine, 1990).
2. See for example, Gould, R, *Enigmas* (London, 1929); Mill, H R, *The Siege of the South Pole* (London, 1905); Mill, W J, *Exploring Polar Frontiers* (Santa Barbara, 2003); Simpson-Housley, P, *Antarctica* (New York, 1992).
3. Druett, Joan, *Hen Frigates: Wives of Merchant Captains under Sail* (London, 1998).
4. See also Druett, p.68.
5. Ibid., pp.60-1.
6. Morrell, Benjamin, Jnr, *A Narrative of Four Voyages* (New York, 1832), pp.350-1.
7. Ibid., pp.379-80.
8. Ibid., p.401.
9. Ibid., p.387.
10. Ibid., p.390.
11. Ambergris is a greyish, waxy substance produced in the digestive system of whales, found on beaches or floating in the sea, and formerly used as a fixative in perfumery.
12. Newell, Harriet, *Memoirs* (Edinburgh, 1817), p.5.
13. Ibid., p.90.
14. Luis vaz de Camoens, sixteenth-century Portuguese poet who wrote *The Lusiad*, an epic poem celebrating Portuguese exploration and discoveries.
15. Vandyke: a linen or lace collar with a zigzag edge, similar to those seen in portraits by the artist Van Dyck, (1599-1641).

SEAFARERS' VOICES

A new series of seafaring memoirs

This new series, Seafarers' Voices, presents a set of abridged and highly readable first-hand accounts of maritime voyaging, in the age of sail which describe life at sea from different viewpoints – naval, mercantile, officer and lower deck, men and women – and cover the years 1700 to the 1900s, from the end of the Mediterranean galleys, through the classic age of sail to the coming of the steamship. Published in chronological order, these memoirs unveil the extraordinary and unfamiliar world of our seafaring ancestors and show how they adapted to the ever-demanding and ever-changing world of ships and the sea, both at war and at peace.

The first titles in the series

For more details visit our website
www.seaforthpublishing.com